Finding God When You Don't Believe in God

Finding God When You Don't Believe in God

Searching for a Power Greater Than Yourself

Jack Erdmann
with Larry Kearney

Foreword by Anne Lamott

■ HAZELDEN®

Hazelden
Center City, Minnesota 55012-0176

1-800-328-0094
1-651-213-4590 (fax)
www.hazelden.org

Library of Congress Cataloging-in-Publication Data
Erdmann, Jack.
    Finding God when you don't believe in God : searching for
  a power greater than yourself / Jack Erdmann with Larry
  Kearney ; foreword by Anne Lamott.
      p. cm.
    ISBN 1-56838-983-3 (pbk.)
    1. Spiritual biography—United States. 2. Alcoholics—
  United States—Biography. I. Kearney, Larry, 1943– II. Title.

  BL72.E73 2003
  291.4'092'2—dc21
  [B]

                                                    2002038896

Editor's note
The stories in this book are based on personal interviews. In some
cases names and certain facts have been changed to ensure
anonymity.

07 06 05 04 03   6 5 4 3 2 1

Cover design by David Spohn
Interior design by Rachel Holscher
Typesetting by Stanton Publication Services, Inc.

For
Peter and Terry Freitas
and
Carol Hill LaRocca

Contents

Foreword

THIS IS THE THIRD BOOK in a series by Jack Erdmann and Larry Kearney. The three, taken together, constitute important and original contributions to the literatures of recovery and spirituality.

The first, *Whiskey's Children,* recounted Erdmann's excruciating journey from a boyhood nearly destroyed by his father's drinking, to a fatherhood in California in which he nearly destroyed his own children, to a hellish alcoholic descent and twenty-five subsequent years of sobriety in the healing community of other sober drunks. It's a book about how you can't get to where Jack is now from where he was, and yet how, one day at a time, he did.

The second book, *A Bar on Every Corner,* described with the same power and insight the specifics of the process—his path through the Twelve Steps of Alcoholics Anonymous from hopelessness to a new life. It's a sometimes funny account of the program—from the belief that the Steps could not work in the face of Jack's unique awfulness, to the gifts promised in the Ninth Step—emotional sobriety, gratitude, and an abiding faith in a Higher Power.

This third book picks up this last theme, and in these interviews with men and women from all walks of life, we hear stories of ordinary, miraculous people. They discuss what they were like, what happened to force them to the point of God, and what it's like now. We hear the truth of the old line that the difference between us and God is that God never thinks he's us. We hear the old thinking that had to be discarded. We see daily faith, and faith in eternity.

One hears in these interviews that the ego-bound mind is the single greatest obstacle to experiencing the presence of grace, of love, of the deep visceral trust in one who has all power and doesn't seem to be you. And that one does not need to turn to the damaged mind for solutions—that there is another way—that there are many other ways.

This book is a choir singing of a faith that matters more than anything and that arrived unexpected after childhoods filled with church doctrine and hypocrisy. There is grief and there is humor, and lots of self-will run riot—if you want to make God laugh, just tell her your plans.

There's Jack Erdmann's own faith walk, from a destructive Catholic upbringing to a commitment to, and from, a loving God.

These are people from different places, different lives, who move out of despair through a Higher Power. Some choose to call it God, and some do not. There are Higher Powers found in other people. There are Higher Powers found in beauty, and one in the basic premise that grace comes with not attaching words to that which cannot be expressed.

And through it all are amazed stories of broken hearts made whole again, and minds quieted in love and wonder. These voices show us various ways to God, or god, or goodness, or presence, or restoration. I believe that anyone who reads this book will come away with the conviction that the door leading to faith is already open. This is a rich, layered, piercing, and sometimes funny song of humanity. It addresses the great question, the great mythic journey, and it is sung by the ordinary and charming voices—those who found the worst in themselves, and then the best.

—ANNE LAMOTT

CHAPTER ONE

The Point of God

THIS ISN'T A BOOK for alcoholics and their families in the sense that *Whiskey's Children* and *A Bar on Every Corner* were. While the alcoholic may have a particular and deep knowledge of what it means to search for a Higher Power, the process is everyone's and is at the core of what it means to be human. Most of us found it a key to both sobriety and being.

Most of us find it difficult to believe that we ever chose to live in that threatening, broken landscape where the "I" is the only eye, and the personality imagines itself as self. We used to live by an effort of the will, by turning and shaking and fingering our lives until the act of thought itself had become tied to pain and regret.

In the aftermath of coming to rest in a sense of God, in the individual's access to God, we found it possible to look at our lives coherently and see ourselves wounded by things over which we had no power, wounded by ourselves and by an idiot insistence on a power we never had. Perhaps it was easier for us, because we were fresh from utter defeat by a substance that didn't care about us one way or the other. We got where we were through our very best thinking, and thought that if we kept doing the same things, we'd keep getting the same results. Our best thinking had got us where we were, and it wasn't good enough.

1

[Look around now—is it good enough?]

So this is a book for everyone. As the poet Jack Spicer once said, "I cannot accord sympathy to anyone who does not recognize the human crisis."

In the seventies, I was reading the paper one morning and came across an ad for a movie called *Ali: Fear Eats the Soul.* I sat looking at it because it seemed to me I'd just seen the truth—fear eats the soul.

The phrase went into my head like an ice pick. I could see my life as a trip into fear and a gradual loss of wholeness. I didn't have much else in those days. Fear and unconsciousness were my two poles. I was reading the paper in the morning, so I must have been sick. Maybe I'd had a drink to lose the shakes; maybe I was trying to get it together to go down the road for a bottle. But there it was in the paper. Fear Eats the Soul. The terrible thing was that the person I'd become, or thought I'd become, was getting a shock of truth from an untrue proposition. True and false had become judgments attached to my single reality of trembling, pain, and fear. Anything that seemed to address that and give it some cosmic dignity had become The Truth, especially if a dollop of self-pity was included.

Fear doesn't eat the soul, though it can feel devoured. The soul can't be eaten, but only muffled. That's what the fear does. It seems the mind looks at the mind until nothing's left but a fugitive memory of wholeness. Yet the soul abides (just the right word), and however faint the voice, it is a voice. Sometimes, when the mind is dreaming in place, you can hear it.

It says simple things and has a presence beyond the voice, a breath of starry night where the skull is nothing at all and doesn't hold us in. It's a Higher Power, both inside us and out in the universe at the same time.

I lived a great portion of my life not hearing or pretending not to hear. My skull was the end of things, and I raged and battered at it. I was afraid of everything that moved, stayed still, or flickered in front of my eyes like a picture in a wind. I was locked inside with alcohol and the illusion of wholeness.

I was the definition of missing. I had a personality (tattered good will, evasion, and please-love-me). I had a mind (fear) and a sense that if I could finally be secret (you don't know me at all), that would be the same as being whole, as long as I had a supply of alcohol. My first experience of wholeness, I thought, was getting drunk. It wasn't. It simply relieved my fear and brought in a rush of relief, luxurious warmth, and simple confidence. It never comes back after the first time, not really, but never mind, never mind, the mind says—be secret, easeful, and drunken. That will do the job.

The astounding thing is that drunks have a hard time imagining a power greater than themselves. They've had the shit beat out of them by a chemical, but "No," they say. "No, not me. I'm not using a crutch."

It's all very sad, though it can be funny, too. I remember a guy who came into a group to tell us that if anyone screwed with his head and tried to get him to believe in God, well, he was out of there.

Nobody said a word and kept to the day's business. He sat there looking belligerent for a while, then gave that up and tried acting aloof. That didn't make it either, so he finally lapsed into skeptical curiosity. He could laugh about it years later.

Some have no problem with the idea of a Higher Power. Not

on the surface, anyway. They have, perhaps, an even greater false pride in that they think they know God and know more about themselves than God does. Weeks in rooms of people who can tell them things they didn't know about themselves is a great corrective.

There are all kinds.

Some don't like to say the word *God.* They're embarrassed. Some think God is the church and can't separate the two. Some just don't care, their minds battered into a place where anything is better than thought.

No wonder some can't handle the word *God,* considering the uses it's been put to. Fortunately, no one has to embrace history in order to reach the substance of love.

In general, the battered, the drunken, and the enslaved are the lucky ones, and if their luck holds, they'll come out on the other side. However, there are people who are alone in their heads and can't quite hear anymore, fearful and angry, rubbed raw but still walking through life like everyone else. They need help, too.

They don't always know there's a problem. They have minds that seem okay. Their emotions may be a little out of whack, and maybe at three in the morning a weight of apprehension comes down and makes it hard to breathe, but overall they manage. If something's missing, if the edges of the hole are sharp and abrasive, well, that's just the Human Condition.

"Yeah," I thought back then. "Fear eats the soul and here I am."

I was wrong. I was wrong about almost everything, though at least in the cases of fear and the soul I was thinking about the right topics.

The drunks in the bar love to talk about big things that never happen. Passion is a dumb show. The real passion is locked in and has more to do with brokenhearted children and dead possibilities. The best a drunk can do is hope to come out the other side, where his thoughts can point him in the right direction.

We're human beings with limits, but fear isn't one of them. The wall at the end of the mind, the breakability of the body, the willingness to inflict—those are limits. Fear is an accretion, an everyday nagging, mental fear, and it empowers cruelty, lies, and evasion. None of which makes us feel good. All of which create more fear of discovery, of payback, of a heart broken for good with the weight of things rushing in like the wind.

The only way out, or in, depending on how you choose to see it, is to come to a point of balance where we're neither taller nor shorter than we are, neither more nor less important. The only way to that place is through a deep acknowledgment of powerlessness.

To see ourselves as powerless can be unpleasant, but it's certainly no stretch. The world now is a map of powerlessness. Bombs are falling everywhere endlessly, and they aren't smart at all.

From the simple acceptance of limited power in any partially controlled setting—a family, a job, a circle of friends— to the overwhelming perception of powerlessness in the face of the universe, we move inevitably and profoundly to the notion of a Higher Power and a place where the mind relaxes gratefully. When we know we're powerless, we're able to do things to make the world better. We fill with grace and hope, without aggression or the trappings of resentment and revenge.

Yes, to make the world better.

This is a book for all of us, remembering what it was like to be a child when the world was a flooding of unknown substance and beauty and all that seemed to be necessary was a motion-less understanding of the whirlwind of codes and expectations.

Is there anyone out there whose earliest memory is wishing for pain? For loneliness, slavery, and solitary resentment? Did any of us want to be told we were unlovable by definition and doomed to misery?

[There are those parents who torment children, God knows, but those kids weren't born to be unlovable and expect every day, God help us, that things might change.]

Things do change. You can go home again, and no matter how the world batters us, it's possible to feel a potential for change in the simple exchange between the love inside and the love outside. Misery and evil are man's entirely and fade to nothing when we wake up, see the morning, and think, "I'm a decent human being and I'll do what I can with my life—for all of us."

Finding a Higher Power is finding a seamless love. It can start with anything outside ourselves. There are drunks who start with a doorknob. Not a bad start at all.

There it is: a Higher Power. It's outside us and inside, doing a better job of existing than we are. It's shiny and cool and fits our hands, and sometimes it's everything we need in the world. What's the big deal? "Please help me, doorknob, from your own perfect being."

Start anywhere. Come to the one place that makes sense and isn't broken. "God," you think, "thank you." Everything leaves the mind and body in the one perfect prayer, which is always "Thank you."

These are first-person stories of how men and women came to the place where whatever bad that happens is understood for what it is—either as an unavoidable working of the natural world or an evil created and maintained by the human mind on its own. The people in this book have different lives and different words but have one thing in common—a God that can't be used to justify cruelty.

They aren't ecstatic, they aren't proselytizers, they aren't eager to compare spiritual states, and they don't want your money. They recognize the grief that comes with the world, and the brooding heartbreak that only God touches by being available to be touched.

There are no thunderbolts here, no sudden awakenings. There are just voices telling stories. If you listen carefully and leave behind the notion that the music has to swell when God makes his entrance, you'll hear grace in these quiet narratives—unashamed and matter-of-fact, as the real thing always is.

I was asked once if I could write a few paragraphs about who God is and what God is like. "Sure," I said, "he's six foot one, looks a bit like Ben Affleck, likes sunsets and long walks on the beach, and he's pleasingly sure of himself."

God is not a being; God is Being. For those who have found God, his presence shows in honesty, kindness, carefully chosen words, and an absence of shame about the past. The pain may still be there, though quieted, but the grandiosity and false ego that insists on either secrecy or great sinnerhood is burned out and gone. They want to pass on what they feel without hype or false drama.

The voices here are so lovely in their gratitude and honesty that listening carefully becomes a privilege. The voices sound with the progression of grace, and one gradually understands that coming to the point of God is just that—coming to a point. Paying attention to life as best one can, moment to moment, can suddenly reveal and open up the place where God is waiting.

If there's a constant in these stories it would seem to be a voice that murmurs and tells the truth in the background and that, as we grow older, can become less hearable in the flux of circumstance. Repeatedly, the violently painful memory of having been someone better once, having wanted nothing but good for everyone, breaks down the assembled personality and lets the soul be heard again. As T. S. Eliot puts it:

> The end of all our exploring
> Will be to arrive where we started
> And know the place for the first time

The memory of who we were and the good we wanted is a memory of God. It's as if we were finally all men and women in shared pain and grace, doing the best we can because we remember God and can do no less.

❧

The first voice you'll hear is Annabella's.

I've known her twenty years. I was working in a residential alcohol program when she came in. She seemed dazed, though her eyes were terribly frightened. She couldn't sleep at all, and in the middle of the night, she'd get up and walk softly down the hall, holding herself with both arms. I found out right away that she couldn't be left alone at night, so I'd listen carefully for her and get up as soon as I heard her door closing. There wasn't much to say. I tried to assure her: "You're okay. You're safe. Let it go for now and see how the morning is. You're tired. Give it up and sleep."

I remember her leaning against the wall by the fish tank. The movement in the tank was vaguely unsettling in the motionless room. She just looked at me, trying to remember where she was.

I figured her chances weren't good. You do that in treatment. Though there's really no predicting, you still try to guess, to minimize your responsibility just in case.

She was looking at me, looking through me at the wall, and I suddenly realized that I would know her for a very long time. I couldn't explain how I knew. I just knew. Which is how it turned out.

In the house, she was quiet with an almost metallic resistance that would show up at odd times, as if a switch had been flipped. She did things wrong. She got drunk once, but came back from that to work slowly and steadily with others, and to try to be what she could.

You want to be who you were before the nightmare started, but you became the person about to get drunk or shoot up. You have to touch the being you were before you built the creaking personality. You have to hear the voice again and see from the old angle, down by the floor, with accurate eyes and nothing but hope.

Annabella moved slowly through it all and came to where she is now. Now her life is at her fingertips and she can offer it to anyone. If there are no trumpets or lilies pushing up through the pavement under her feet, that's because the progression of grace is seamless. One hardly knows. All that counts is the attention, so that now and then the brightness shows through and fills the place with nothing but God.

Annabella is in her mid-forties with a strong, high-cheek-boned Sicilian face, soft eyes, and dark brown hair she wears curved into the back of her neck.

Her house is on Staten Island, and there's a flat expanse of marsh and water beyond the glass, deepening in the April afternoon light. Just outside the door, a mockingbird is perched at the top of a picnic table umbrella.

She has two children, ages fifteen and five. She's a therapist and works at a residential alcohol/drug program where women and their children can be safe during treatment.

She has a soft alto voice and an easy way of talking emotionally about what she's learned through her twenty years of sobriety and helping others. If you can't talk about your feelings, it's hard to stay straight. She talks about her life. Her face is quiet normally, almost expressionless, though benign and dignified. When she smiles, it's a lovely thing.

CHAPTER TWO

Annabella

WELL, I WAS BORN here in 1954. My family were restaurant people, down on Hylan Boulevard. My grandmother, my mother's mother, owned the restaurant, and my father had built it up for years. My grandmother was a lot like me. I always felt connected to her, and even more when she died. I have a beautiful picture of her at sixteen, dressed in traditional peasant clothes, very poised and self-possessed—womanly.

Her daughter, my mother, married my father, a decent and kind man. I loved him very much. When he died, I seemed to have lost everything. I was completely alone. At his funeral, out of control on alcohol and drugs, I made a scene at the church. I remember the family looking at me. For me, they weren't really even there. There wasn't anything there but me and my dead father. I couldn't have reached them at all, even if I had wanted to.

That was at Saint Anselm's, the center of everything that happened in the family, like christenings and weddings.

To me it had been just another fancy building. It still is, I guess, though I do go into a church every once in a while just to sit in the quiet and think or pray.

My father had been everything to me. He'd been like a safe harbor. I have two brothers and a sister; I was the youngest. My mother, all the women in the family, were very Sicilian in that they deferred to the men as a matter of course. They did have power, but they didn't have to show it. My mother had more power over me than I like to think about. Every time I opened a door, there she was.

My earliest memories are the Sunday afternoon get-togethers for lunch with all my cousins running around. I always spent a lot of time with my father. I remember being with him at the restaurant and eating steamed clams. I remember going with him to the dump once a week. For some reason he refused to pay for garbage pickup. So once a week we'd drive together to the dump. Very Sicilian, I guess.

We'd sneak down to the restaurant's Dumpster in the dark, and he'd tell me to stand guard. I felt very important and proud. He'd get the garbage from the trunk and throw it in, and then we'd drive away quietly with the lights out.

My mother was a disordered woman. Whatever was stable and solid seemed to break in her hands. She thrived on that, pulling the rug out from under us so we didn't have a place to stand, couldn't predict anything, didn't know what was going to happen, or what she was going to say. She was the opposite of my father, who always tried to give us a place to be where we knew we were loved. I could feel that from him, though he wasn't willing to stand against my mother. I think he was too tired and needed to come home and be quiet. He just couldn't face it.

She made all of us go to church every Sunday, but she didn't go herself. The church was where we heard that if we were feeling guilty, that's how we should be feeling. There wasn't any space to breathe in what we learned, and the priests were guys in black with quirks and lives of their own. They were unpredictable just like everyone else. They had power over us, and they rubbed it in.

This big, empty, quiet church with statues, candles, and stone was very beautiful. But what came out of the priests was original sin and you're guilty, you're damned. We were children. What had we done? At home, my mother told me the same thing.

Nothing is worse than a brutalized child who doesn't understand what the point is, which is how all brutalized children are. A child looks and looks and tries to understand, but there's nothing to hold on to. Everybody says mothers love their kids, so you have to be wrong. It has to be you there's something wrong with.

There were two separate places in my life—my father's safe harbor, where I was lovable, and my mother's desert, where I was a worthless disappointment. I was too fat, she said. I was homely, unfeminine. I was wrong in everything.

I was alone. I had to make everything up because what was real wasn't doing anything for me. Every time I saw my mother, I tensed. Her words came out like fists, and I couldn't get away. I was overweight and shouldn't eat candy, but candy was all I felt I had. I'd hide it in my room and eat candy at night, alone in the dark.

I was getting crazy. I was pulling as far back as I could get. I didn't have a rosy fantasy life—everything was as terrible as ever—but it's like I was making myself a little slower to respond, a little less able to hear the words and feel them right away. When I didn't want to hear I could get confused.

The family wasn't together much. Everybody worked down at the restaurant. Only on Thursday nights we'd all have dinner together. I remember the night the restaurant burned down. My older brother picked up my sister and me and drove us down to see. The street was a sheet of water; the flames glowed orange in it. I was four or five, I guess. We'd just moved into our new house. I loved the big closet in my room. Inside, it had a little window where the sun came through. It was so warm and so secret in there. I'd sit there for hours.

My mother used to dye my hair in the bathtub to make it look like hers. It was very long, but she cut it off short and put the long tresses in cellophane in her closet. She said she was going to have a hairpiece made.

I got left back in second grade because I couldn't see the blackboard. I couldn't stand up to read because I was so self-conscious. All I could feel was eyes on me. My voice wouldn't work at all. So I repeated second grade, and all my cousins went to the third. That was it. I was stupid.

When they finally found out I couldn't see—my uncle noticed how I'd bring a forkful of spaghetti all the way up to my eyes before putting it into my mouth—thick glasses were added to my face, which I already thought nobody liked.

By the time I was eleven, all I had was a bunch of crazy adaptations and avoidances. My mother was sick, on top of everything else. One night at home, we were there alone. She started screaming at me about something or other and fell on the floor and started to bleed. I didn't know what to do. It was obviously my fault, I thought. I'd made her bleed. I called my father at the wharf, crying, saying, "Mommy is bleeding all over everything."

The ambulance came, and she had a hysterectomy.

Everything went on and on. All my pleasures became secret things I'd do alone. Except for sports, and that was doomed. I should have known it would be. One day I was trying to get the guys at the school field to let me play baseball with them. Someone called my mother. She found me playing ball in the street with some boys and grabbed me, shrieking that I was a disgrace and an embarrassment to her, and that she didn't want to be seen with me.

By seventh grade, I was stealing my father's cigarettes and smoking them on the way home from school. I was seen smoking in the street in my school uniform, and the principal brought me to her office and asked me about it. I denied smoking and said something smart (I'd started doing that). She smacked me across the face.

There are holes in my memory, but there's this dead sense of simple unhappiness. And confusion. I couldn't quite understand what the problem was or how I'd got to be so miserable.

It had to be my fault. Other kids weren't like me, and if you're not like other kids, and your mother doesn't want to be seen with you, well, it's who you are.

Did God love me? Who knew? I wasn't lovable, so the odds weren't good. I thought to ask God for help, but I wasn't good at asking for help. Asking for help from the priests was out of the question.

I was learning to take care of myself, I thought. I was a troubled adolescent girl. I listened to pop music and hid candy bars in my room. Nothing that was going on seemed to be available to me. I wasn't one of the girls in the songs (maybe the girl in the one that went "Knock three times on the ceiling if you want me"). My father loved me. My sister Susan tried to take care of me.

There was something else, too. Years later, when I was already in treatment, I went home for a weekend. Everyone was talking about the past. My mother said, "There was that time you disappeared and we were so terrified." She told a story about how I'd been with my father in the drugstore and disappeared. They'd been out frantically looking for me, and my father had found me coming out of a building with some strange man who said he'd found me wandering around. They'd asked me, and I'd said, "No. Nothing happened." What could have happened? I was five years old and already shell-shocked; I wouldn't have known what to say. They'd brought me home.

There I was, on my first pass from treatment, sitting at the dinner table with everyone remembering but me.

Adolescence was like walking into a minefield. The softball thing was a nightmare. Even when I did well, like playing with the local girls' softball team, I was still wrong.

My mother said softball wasn't feminine. She said I was an embarrassment to everyone and that she barely wanted to let me be seen on the street. I guess my father knew how it was. I don't really know. He couldn't do much, anyway. That's how things were.

Oddly enough, I can be with my mother now. We don't talk about anything that happened. Maybe we don't really talk about much at all, but there's something else in my life now. I exist in a different place, and I don't have to hate her. I don't need revenge, which is a powerful thing. This different place is where I can feel real and at peace.

I remember how excited we all were about confirmation in second grade. We'd get to wear white dress and veils and be important. I went with my mother, of course, to get the dress. They had to let the dress out. "Nothing is ever simple with you," she said.

Children have a natural reverence, I believe. They know about mysteries, and they get excited about things like confirmation. When it happens, though, it's all about the dress, how you look, how the other kids look, and who's the prettiest. I don't think we give kids much to be reverential about.

After two months in high school, I started using alcohol and marijuana and ended up in a psych unit where we all slept on mattresses on the floor. I remember trying to cut my wrist with my name bracelet.

It wasn't just the old high school stuff that had got me there. I'd been so angry—possessed by anger. I knew I had to get out of the house, so I ran away once, but that didn't work. I lit a couple of small fires in the basement. Then there was a family conference, and the males, all my uncles, sat around and talked about me. That's how it was in a Sicilian household. They decided I needed psychiatric treatment.

I remember us driving out on the Belt Parkway, out on Long Island. I didn't know where we were going because no one had told me. We walked in the front door, and there was a large man, bald, with a mustache, standing in front of us. He was my psychiatrist. I asked him why he was staring at me.

I was supposed to go to the children's ward, but no room was available there, so they put me in with the adults. I was thirteen. I hadn't even known I was being sent to the hospital.

I was there two days. There were women talking pointlessly to themselves. Some were screaming. I was terrified. I called my father, and he came to take me home. He arranged for me to see a psychiatrist twice a week before school. I'd take a bus to his office, then a bus back to school. I eventually ran away again and went to the convent, where I met a sister I could trust. I asked for her help.

I saw the church as a sanctuary. Whether or not it had anything to do with God didn't really matter to me. Nothing is worse for a child's sense of God than watching the hypocrisy all around. The way people were in church wasn't the way they were outside in the world. Were they God's people? Where was God, anyway? I wasn't a bad person. I'd never been a bad person. I was a confused little girl who wasn't so little anymore.

My father, I guess, was an image of God, but he had never been there. Most of the time, he'd been working long hours. When he'd come home, my mother would tell him, in a reasonable way, in a different voice, all the terrible things I'd done. I guess he believed her.

It's odd how the scenes from my early childhood are clear and my parents stand out, but as I get into adolescence and things get really bad, my memory blurs. Maybe because I was medicated all the time.

I went to a bunch of different schools. Saint Joseph's stands out, a residential Catholic school for troubled girls. Once I stole a school car with another girl and we drove to Nyack, came back, and turned ourselves in to the police.

I spent the night in Juvenile Hall. I can still remember that room. It was so cold. The one window had been painted over with white paint. When you're very angry, very young, and very scared, you're on a treadmill.

They took me back at Saint Joseph's. One night, I went to Sister Mary Edward's room to ask for a sleeping medication because I felt lonely and couldn't sleep. She took me into her bed. The only thing I remember clearly is her leaning over to kiss me and put her tongue in my mouth. I ran away again, but I was brought back. This time I got out by starting another small, pointless fire. I was sent back to Pilgrim State. I was sixteen, and I'd be there till I was almost nineteen. It wasn't good at all.

I was angrier than it's possible for a young girl to be. Under my anger was a grief so intense it could eat me alive if I let it. The anger was better.

They pumped me full of Prolixin and tied me to beds. All I could think was, "This isn't me."

Psychiatry was largely a matter of learning to keep my mouth shut while seeming to talk. I'd sit in there, just the psychiatrist and me, and I'd figure out what he wanted to hear and feed it to him. It was almost like he was a patient who needed to hear certain things to stay well.

I went to school on the grounds, but it wasn't much of a school. I learned next to nothing. I was seventeen and I'd never really had schooling. The whole progression of my education threw me into self-consciousness. In class, a nun went on and on in front of a blackboard. Now, it was a roomful of kids in various stages of madness, without the nun.

There were family sessions with the psychiatrist, and finally my parents walked out on me. My father left because he couldn't take the things I was saying to my mother (it was all the truth; I thought telling the truth was what I was supposed to do). "You are not my daughter," my mother said. She got up, took her purse, and left.

It was what they call "closure," I guess. That's a stupid word. There are no closures, only human beings moving from one direction to another.

I guess I prayed when things got bad at Pilgrim State. There's a lot I don't remember. It's okay. I don't want to remember, and I know there wasn't much there. God was there, as always, but I was locked so deep in my head I could barely see out.

At Christmastime when I was eighteen, my mother and father came up to give me a present. I hadn't heard from them at all, but there they were with a Christmas present. I wouldn't see them. It was the first time I'd ever set a boundary between us.

I had my first sexual experience at Pilgrim State. It was degrading, just what you would expect. When I thought I was going to get out because I'd been submissive, with all the right answers, they didn't let me go. My anger just snapped, and I ran away with another girl.

Within a matter of hours, we were back in the hospital. Tied down to a bed again, locked in a closet, kept in pajamas so I couldn't go anywhere.

I remember now a staff person named Jerry. I had been given too much Prolixin and spent a whole day with my head twisted back on my neck so I could only look at the ceiling. When I came down, I was at the bottom of everything and could only sit passively. Jerry brought me a hamburger he'd got from a restaurant and tried very gently to get me to eat. In the three years at Pilgrim State, that's the one piece of kindness I really remember.

I was almost nineteen when they told me I could go home. There wasn't any home, of course, but they were opening the door. It was terrifying, but it was what I wanted. I went outside with a sad kind of shell around me and an expressionless face.

I rented a room in Islip. I remember walking out the front door. It was spring and a nice day. The sun was warm, and I felt like it was my first free day, ever. I said the word *free* out loud.

Free. My God. I didn't know anything. I had no family except for an agonizing set of memories. I had no schooling. I was entirely artificial and defensive. That's what you learn in the hospital.

I had one friendship with a psych tech from the adolescent unit, and I ended up living with her. She was an alcoholic, and from that day forward everything begins to be the same. Because when you're addicted, everything dissolves into "When is the next drink?" Whatever else seems to be going on is just a show.

I don't have a lot to say about those years. I've told the story a lot. After a while it's just a simpleminded refrain. You can barely believe it—the boredom, the misery, the lies that screen you off. It doesn't hurt to remember so much as it is embarrassing. Everything you ever did is tainted and humiliating.

I went to school, got my license, and went back to Pilgrim State to work as a psych tech. My father was proud. He bought me a house. That hurts, because he loved me and I threw it all away.

At the hospital, we'd been getting through the night shifts with chemical help. After a year or so, I was seriously addicted to speed, along with the ever-present alcohol. I was making good money but usually couldn't pay my $270 mortgage at the end of the month.

I was about twenty-five when I tried to kill myself. I overdosed, but a friend stopped by unexpectedly and got me to the hospital. The doctor told me I died and came back. I do remember a light and a profound comfort, just like the others. It did nothing for me, though, because I was locked in and alone. I was as angry at God as it was possible to be, considering that I barely believed.

The light wasn't enough. When I woke up, I was tied down and hallucinating. Ants were crawling on me. Being alive was too much for me. I wasn't connected to anyone, at least not on the surface, which was all that was left.

I never expected to live past twenty-six. Why that age, I couldn't tell you. Instead of me, my father died when I was twenty-six. I stayed alive, but he was dead. There wasn't anyone else in my life. The only sense of positive self I had was tied up with him, and now he was gone.

When I'd got out of the hospital he was there for me, all the time, with whatever I needed, whatever help he could offer. He'd drive up with food. He let me talk to him.

The morning he died, I was feeling shaky. I'd gone home early and drunk myself to sleep. My brother called to say my father was dead, and I thought, "Why hadn't it been Mom?" The first thing I did was call a friend for some dope.

I disgraced myself at the funeral and went back to Islip having reached the bottom of everything, I thought. But there's always, almost always, another step down from where you are. I was perfectly ready to take that step, so I sold the house my father had bought for me with such high hopes.

I bought a bar with the money, lived above it, and pretended I was on top of everything. I sold his house for a bar. I remember some of the faces and the apartment where I gradually lost my mind, but most of it is a haze. It was all dark except for the lights inside the big mirror. I was good at running a bar. I had two sets of books. I was finding out that I was competent, that I could do things, but what you learn when your mind is toxic doesn't stick. When you come down you've learned nothing.

I learned how to dress for the nights in the bar. I learned how to present myself so that if I wanted company for the night, I could get it easily enough. It was all pretenses. All illusion. I wasn't competent. I was a sad little girl in a dangerous place.

It's a haze. There was the lit-up sign, White Horse Inn, a neon jukebox, a gravel parking lot next to the highway, and a flight of stairs up the side of the building to my apartment. I had a big carved dark wood waterbed in a small apartment where all my alcohol and drugs were.

I lasted six months.

I was lucky enough to reach a place where I'd emptied myself of most everything. I was alive, but that's all. I existed as a thing with needs. Where are my drugs? Where is my liquor? I call it lucky because it's what got me to where I am.

Nothing at all was left in my world but misery and fear. Not dying forced me to do *something*. I don't take that as a special gift. I think it's a gift that's always there. We think we don't need it or are too clogged with rage or resentment and can't do anything. But when you get to the place where it's all gone, except for you and an empty world, things happen.

If you don't die, you do something.

Toward the end of my six months at the White Horse, I was alone upstairs holding a shotgun and hiding behind the curtain on the back living-room window. There was a moon and music coming up through the floor, a kind of thumping, and out on the roof were police in the moonlight, just sitting there, waiting for me.

I'd been selling drugs over the bar. I'd been holding poker games upstairs. I'd been talking to undercover cops. Rick was my best friend, and I'd got him jail time by talking stupidly to a cop. They were out on the roof waiting for me. I had a shotgun and nothing in my head but fear.

They weren't really there but they had been. It was as real as anything else, and something in it worked for me. I don't know what it was. I just know that soon afterward I went into treatment about forty miles away.

How did that happen? I don't know. I was barely a conscious being. I had nerves and not much else. I said good-bye to everyone and told them I was going in for surgery (maybe I really was). I thought I'd be back. I was just going to get straight and come back so I could live the same life but now in an orderly fashion.

I was a wreck the first week. The house manager was awake most of the nights, talking to me and keeping me away from sharp things. I remember the dark house at three in the morning, the couch in the little waiting room, the old windows.

It was odd the way I looked at things. I was hopeless and I had hope. It didn't make any sense that one minute I thought I had to die and the next I knew that I could stay alive. Gradually there was the sense that the house, the whole place, was making an effort at love. We were trying to love each other.

That was the Higher Power everyone was talking about. On the wall on a poster were the words "Came to believe that a power greater than ourselves could restore us to sanity." It wasn't one of the silk-sheet treatment centers with drugs to come down on and spectacular views. It was an old house on a little hill in San Rafael. The staff were all recovering, spiritual people, and the clients were the real thing—down and out and ready to die.

We all asked for help, or all of us who could. It was very difficult and strange for me to ask for help, but the help came. There was a gradual flooding of something I didn't know about. It seemed to come most strongly when something good had happened, after someone had been helped or had come to a place where they could say things they'd never said before.

We all tried to tell the truth and sometimes succeeded.

It was a routine of getting up, getting clean, and working hard. There was a sense of time itself being special—"Here, you've been given this time. Do something with it."

Thinking about going back to the bar made me afraid. I didn't want to because I knew I'd never make it if I did. After the fourth week I was in the program, the bar burned down. It was the most delicate gift I'd ever been given. No one was hurt and the bar was gone. I didn't have insurance to cover it, but it didn't matter. I drove up there with the house manager and looked in my charred apartment. There was nothing to take back, only a few small things my father had given me. Nothing else.

I was free. Driving back, I felt all right. It was never something all at once. I know people who have had revelations and suddenly changed, but not me. It was a process. It moved slowly, and sometimes I found myself back in the hospital, acting out. That didn't matter because underneath everything, underneath all of us, was this solid floor and a need to love each other because we were going to survive.

It didn't even matter whether or not life was fake on some days. When it was, you could feel the fakery and learn that it wouldn't work.

That was twenty-one years ago. I'm here now because I was shown where God's grace was, and it gave me the strength to endure. Not all at once.

AA uses the words *Higher Power,* but it's always just been God to me. I don't go to church. I don't consider myself much of a Catholic, but every day my life is filled with knowing that when I find myself lost or empty, there's a place I can go that holds nothing but love, a safe place that doesn't guarantee me anything but the strength to go on. It doesn't have to. The certainty of the love is everything.

My mother's okay. Sad to say, she probably did her best. My children are the visible signs of God to me. Now I have what I've always cared about, some sort of real home, I guess, a place where love flows back and forth. The first time I held my first son, I knew that there wasn't anything else but love, and that if I'd been able to give up earlier, things could have been different.

What would I want to be different?

No revelation, just process. It was finding a Higher Power, but

I don't describe it that way, because when I came into treatment everything in the world was higher. Finding a Higher Power involves other people, joining them consciously. Probably it comes mostly from giving up. When you've really got nothing, and everything you thought was you is cheap and flimsy, you can only pray, "Oh God, please help me." You mean it and give up. You wait to see what happens.

A counselor I loved named Harry M. told me, "Throw everything away and the real stuff will come floating back." He treated me like I was his daughter, and I listened to him.

When my grandmother was dying last year, my sister and I were with her in her room in the middle of the night. We were both praying she could finally just die; it had been so long and hard for her. She had a fierce will, but finally she did die. There was a clear smell of gardenias in the room. It was her favorite flower because her dead husband had given her gardenias when they were married. I asked my sister and she smelled it too. It was very plain.

It was the way everything seems to me now—ordinary and impossible at the same time.

CHAPTER THREE

Please Help Me

I'M SITTING HERE at three in the morning, and it's dark and cold. I remember how it used to be at three in the morning, when I'd wake and stumble downstairs for a drink to stop me from shaking at the enormity of being human, conscious, and in pain forever.

Now it's cold and dark. I can hear the planet turning out there, through the windows and across the flimsy buildings and out to the edges where the clouds are giant streaming ghosts with stars above in a great empty beauty.

There are beings all around in the dark, and the differences between us are minimal—a slight rearrangement of genes, a different set of faces in the head. All across the ragged edges of a big rocky ball are minds in disarray and flux, sleeping or waking, trying to understand.

Is it my fault? Did I do it? No, it isn't my fault. It's them. No, all I have to do is be different, do things differently, and I can make it right again. It was right once, wasn't it? When was that? I could feel it then, but now my brain won't go there. I came from somewhere and here I am, and it's dark and cold. The sun will be up in three hours. What should I do till then? Kill the goddamn fear. That's the thing. Kill the way I am.

Creak and groan, and the planet rolls over in the dark.

Here I am still, though something is different from the way

it used to be. There's a sense of the lights in the houses, the few lights, and the web of the human, all of us barely different from each other, trying as hard as we can. And the hugeness of things. Even here, in the room with the orange light from the invented lamp shining on the invented computer screen and the white tea cup and my fingers aged to about sixty and the far corners of the made-up room, tumbling with the planet through the dark, one horizon up, one horizon down.

What's different is that I'm in love. I always was, but didn't realize it. So deeply in love that trying to move away from it was like a kid trying to run between the raindrops.

I look back because memory is a much misunderstood and all-encompassing tool. I look back and understand that probably it took precisely the things I did to get me here. Here is not a bad place. I'm not always proud that I've come to a place where I can roll through space in the dark and feel grateful. At times, I caused enormous pain to others, to people I loved or claimed to love, and battered them with my vanity and fear. All of that is with me. I cringe sometimes just walking down the street. However, something is different. People are born, people die, and for a brief time they're here and trying as hard as they can with damaged materials and doubtful tools. They're me. And I pray with them as surely as if I were lost again on the street, making my way through the crowds and astonished at all the eyes shining and moving, looking at me and looking away. I pray by saying, "These are me." It's a great relief.

And "Please help me," I sometimes say, as I would have once said, "Sing for me, muse?" I'm not really talking to anyone. It's a habit I got into when I was very sick and needed help but couldn't bring myself to ask. It was odd—the way I was. I couldn't just say, "I need help." It was a matter of pride, I guess. False pride is a terrible thing, and it kills. I remember the way I tried to hold my head up in the treatment program interview. Holding up my head was a tacit lie, and they told me later it was painful to watch.

We cross a line and appear from out of the dark. Then we cross it again and disappear into the dark. In between, we flail and break each other down, knowing all the time that something is wrong, that things should be different. We pass along misery and fear as if they were family traditions. We become willing to increase the misery of children for money and power. We look at ordinary, vicious venality masquerading as wealth and position, and think, "Well, he must be doing something right." We take what we think is the easier, softer way, and it turns out to be the font of misery.

It's three-thirty now, and the tea is half gone. All I need in this world is to get this right. That's not true, of course. I need a lot of other things, but when you're trying to address God, it's good to get it right.

Not that I think God cares.

I cringe when I hear God's lists of attributes. He's powerful, merciful, takes offense easily, throws his enemies into the flames, and changes his mind. So watch out.

These are the attributes of a relatively benign warlord. God is God, and his being is being, and his single attribute is the love that isn't human at all. It fills the universe like a perfectly still thought.

We go to the backs of our brains, and there's a sign that says "God" or "End of the line." In the fronts of our brains our eyes are throwing images of a vastness so beautiful and impossible and inescapable that there's nowhere to go but to the notion of heaven.

"Please help me to get this right," I pray.

"Where does it hurt?" we ask our children, but we know already. We know the voice that heals and draws together and the one that cracks, shrieks, and inflicts. We plod along and pass the misery. All the while, we know God is at the back of our minds, where they end, and in the front, where the world is unimaginable.

Human beings are human beings, the world is the world, and when a rock falls on you, it's always going to hurt. Though it is impossible not to feel the pain and fall into despair, it is possible not to pass it on.

When finished, Annabella's story created a presence in the room. Uncontained, it went out in all directions because the voice was right, and told the best truth it knew how to tell. She didn't say the world was wonderful, or that she'd been chosen by God, or that there was no pain to come, or that she'd always rise above it. Instead, she said that when she gave up and put her head down, strength came to her. The core of the strength was a love beyond her understanding.

She didn't have to talk about belief, because she knew that in the presence of grace, belief isn't a factor anymore. You cannot believe and still be in God. You can turn your mind off entirely and still be in God. That's a wonderful thing. Because what's most useful in belief is disbelief, which brings you closer to God as you try to sustain it, which is a form of obsession with God. Belief itself is of the mind and can go in any direction, toward any cruelty.

We find out the inadequacy of the mind more readily through nonbelief than belief.

There was just something for Annabella to pass along, so she did.

When I was a kid and relatives would come to visit us, some-one would always slip a dollar into my hand. The feeling of it had nothing to do with the dollar, or what it could buy. It had to do with the simple continuity of passing things along, like the old songs they used to sing at parties—the voices equal, good or bad.

Passing God along is like that. Every time you give it away, you can feel God—apart from the twistings of rationality, belief, and the human construction of God as man writ large.

The perfect, heartbreaking thing is that you find that there is no entropy in the passing on of love. It never runs down or diminishes.

It's a wonderful thing to learn.

At AA meetings, people know to pass along what they have. It's how they stay sober. One thing you hear repeatedly in the offered stories is the sadness and anger of the child in the church of the parents, empty and frightened in the place where God was supposed to live.

A child's heart goes out to places of mystery naturally, but despite all the lovely stonework, woodwork, metalwork, and sweet bells, the church door may open on nothing but adults in a palace of vanity.

I picture Annabella at eight years old, wearing her uniform, tenderhearted and confused, having to leave grace behind when she went to the place where it was supposed to live.

I'm sure there are real churches where children aren't killed in their hearts. But when you hear the stories of the men and women newly back from despair, it's hard to say.

I look at Annabella, her head turned to the light on the water, and I wonder why she was thrown away. Is it a difficult thing to understand that a child's heart goes out to the unknown trust-ingly, and doesn't deserve to be wounded?

Unbearable emotions leave holes that have to be filled. Kill the pain at all cost, the mind says. Kill the pain at all cost and be secret, because if you're a secret they can't find you to hurt you. Be secret and be strong. Don't give up, because that's what they want. The most unsightly wino on the street is possessed of enormous, sterile, unreal strength.

But the strength that comes with surrender is different. It's the strength to accept, endure, and love without infliction.

Power involves infliction. Power kills as a matter of course.

Annabella still sometimes has the voice of a child a little afraid of being corrected, a little conscious that she's lost things before through too much honesty. Nevertheless, she talks anyway. The ones who have come to understand all have that in common. They may be scared, but they talk anyway.

It's still dark and cold here, and I really need to warm up my tea. The sun will come up, and maybe I'll see it direct or maybe we'll be fogged in again. Here by the water there's white all over everything in the mornings, thinner here, thicker there.

"Please help me," I say.

❧

The next voice is Peter's. He's dead now, but you can still hear him.

CHAPTER FOUR

Peter

IN MARCH OF '99, two months before his twenty-fifth birthday, my oldest son, Terry, was murdered in Colombia. Two others were with him. They were Indian rights activists. I think about it and deal with the grief every day, and my strength comes from nowhere.

I can look with my mind and say, "Why bother?" but the strength keeps me going anyway. You wonder how you got to where you are. It's like you think, "Jesus, I'd never get through that," watching someone else, and then you're in it, too, and something happens.

"How do I stand this?" I say to myself, when I notice.

I was a shy kid and always tried to pick the ways that would lead to peace and quiet, but it never worked.

My parents got divorced early on, and it either woke me up or put me to sleep. I'm not sure which. That doesn't make much sense. It was dramatic. I lived with my mother at first as she moved through various rooms, apartments, jobs, and social lives.

Part of the time we stayed with a woman in Corte Madera who drank. I remember she had red hair. We moved to a duplex that had a yard with a rope swing, and I stayed on it for hours. If I swung high, I could see over the tall hedge to the woods and the country lanes. I had a sense that the woods were waiting for me. I thought a lot about what might be waiting for me. Things had always been unstable at home. I used to walk to school with Susie, a pretty little blond girl, and I remember wishing that I could always be right there with her.

Mom would be asked to sing at the Starlite Club, an art deco palace perched on the side of a hill over Highway 101. It had been a giant StarKist tuna can at the World's Fair on Treasure Island. It now had sheets of dark glass and was all black and blue inside. They were slanted outward, and there were angled steel struts outside. I liked it there.

My mom was a maintenance drinker, and Dad seemed to have a dead-end life.

Sometimes he'd take me to the carnival on Saturday mornings or to the gym to interest me in boxing. I was a scrawny kid, but he tried. He'd feed me big breakfasts in the under-construction house he shared with a sheet metal worker named Max.

I loved those breakfasts. There was a lot of good feeling there. When Dad remarried, I moved in with him. I was a new-comer kid in the neighborhood, and I got roughed up.

I learned to do solitary things. I learned to draw by myself. I drew constantly. I didn't have anyone to worry about while I was drawing. I didn't have anybody to please.

I got good grades when I was young, but gradually I found a need to be popular and forgot about the grades. I remember a kid named J. C. Morris grinning as he stole my basketball. After-ward, I didn't want to be that isolated kid anymore. So I con-sciously pursued being popular. I was the friend of the jocks and the wise guys. I entertained in class and drew cartoons.

Dad built us a house in a suburban neighborhood. I combed my hair like Ricky Nelson, but we weren't the family in *Ozzie and Harriet*. I wanted us to be, but nobody was. It was an ideal.

I liked Don Sherwood a lot, too, the early morning guy on KSFO radio. He talked about his drinking and hit out at pomp and authority. Ozzie and Harriet meet the Wolf Man.

I had two sets of emotions in my head. I had nowhere to go at all, but everything I wanted seemed to be a place. If I could find this place I wouldn't have to feel the way I did. I remember my mother singing "I'll Be Seeing You," and that song would hint at where I could go, but not for long. The song or feeling never stayed.

The Starlite was a fancy bar, anyway. When everything was over, early in the dark mornings, there'd be Juanita's Gallery for breakfast or the Charles Van Damme ferry in Sausalito. The Starlite looked out over the San Francisco Bay and all the lights.

When my father married again and I lived with them, I didn't much care about my stepmother. Maybe I did, but if I did, I didn't let myself feel it. We rubbed each other the wrong way.

I went deeper into myself. I was the kind of kid who expected some big change where everything would be better. Things changed, didn't they? Maybe I'd walk out of the door one morning, and there'd be an alien craft to take me aboard. An alien would simply announce, "Hey, come aboard. It was all just an experiment."

I thought of my stepmother as an experiment. My real life was still with my mother. I remember when I was even younger, Dad and Grandpa came home one evening when I was sitting playing with dirt by the curb. Grandpa asked me what was I building, and I said, "It's San Quentin." He said, "Why not make a church instead?"

That was a strange thing to say. It stayed with me. You remember this stuff and finally it all seems to be meaningful in an odd way, out of ordinary time, and always right there in memory. Why was I building San Quentin? It was a good question. I don't know the answer to that one.

At night, I would stare at the moon and stars. I always knew something was out there. Whether or not it would help me was another matter. Grandmother, during one of our last visits together, said simply, "You just try and be the best person you can be when it comes to how you treat other people."

Maybe my stepmother was a roadblock, but what would I have known or been if she'd been different? We were two personality types who simply rubbed each other the wrong way.

I've accused her of being the least spiritual of all the church-going women I ever knew, but she knew about gratitude and I didn't. She knew all about gratitude—that doing things for others was the surefire way to deflate one's own ego. Wherever she got that, she was right.

Information was coming from everywhere, but I needed a place to listen, a place to be safe and self-contained. That's what I thought.

Later I'd meet hardworking atheists, in and out of the program, who worked as hard at proving the nonexistence of God as those who were working on faith. I don't know that there's any way to work on this stuff. I think if you're working on it, all you end up with is a lonely mind, walking in a circle. Like I worked and worked on dealing with my son's death—hard work.

The stuff that keeps me alive comes on its own.

I used to have plenty of substitutes before. All the paths I picked seemed to lead to peace and quiet, but none of them did. Still, at least I was looking for something.

When I looked in the mirror and my hair was fixed just right, like Ricky Nelson, I thought maybe there was a way to handle the world. Maybe I could make things stay still and be all right. I loved things that would fill the time with expected stuff, good humor, and always be there.

It seemed to me that as I got older, the R & B station out of Oakland was saving my life. That's how it felt, listening in the dark. I could always go into the music and there'd always be my bed to listen in. I remember going to the Cow Palace to see Elvis.

Once in my uncle Ernie's car, Elvis came on the radio singing "Heartbreak Hotel," and Ernie started to change the station. I jumped in my seat and shouted, "What the hell do you think you're doing?"

Older still, I hung out with my cousin, Fast Freddie, a member of the Swanx. He had a 1940 LaSalle Coupe, low to the ground, and I gained a rep because everybody knew Freddie. We all got together at the King Cotton Drive-In. We had a hotrod and streetfighting club, and we organized drag races out on San Quentin stretch.

I was moody and quiet, but I tried to talk to girls, and I dressed cool.

If I wasn't who I wanted to be, at least I could be on top of it. If everybody thought I was who I pretended to be, maybe I could make that work for me. I had a last name that was well known in the county, and everyone figured I was a rich kid from this dairy ranching family. Everybody believed I was one of them, the rich people, and that I had it made because I had money. It wasn't true. We were blue collar all the way.

There were two things by then that I really wanted—to play the piano like Fats Domino and to be a drunk. Another kid took the first job, so I practiced the second.

Being a drunk would give me all the cool I needed. Mostly it was a way you could stop time. Alcohol would always be there, like KLIB on the radio. I could go to a place where I'd be cool and private, and if anything happened I could look at it slow and not get rattled.

On a few beers, with the smell of lacquer in my nose, I had a good steady hand. I ran flame jobs and pinstripes on local rods. I became a real good drinker. My mother's new husband had given me lessons in how to drink without throwing up. Who the hell was he? Just somebody else the world had thrown into my life. He was no one, but he didn't know.

During the sixties, I drove cab in the city while I went to art school. I was always high because it helped me talk up the fares. Everyone wanted to go to North Beach, Big Al's, and Finocchio's. Conventioneers, high rollers, merchant seamen, hookers. Sometimes I'd get a call to pick up and deliver a bottle to some darkened living room in Pacifica.

I got good enough with my art to get a job and moved down to Los Angeles, where my paycheck afforded me cocaine, too. I had become a drunk and a drug addict, but it wasn't like I hadn't wanted it. I worked the corporate media—television, advertising, some publishing.

We weren't selling out—we talked about the Zen quality of TV ads, the effort and the money that would go into images that flickered and disappeared. We figured we were Kafkaesque. I sometimes thought of myself drunkenly as Rimbaud, dealing arms in the heart of the darkness. It was all pretty sad.

I married, had kids, and got divorced. I was an L.A. guy. When the kids were grown, I went back to Marin where the air was still clean and nothing looked like the San Fernando Valley yet.

By then, I'd been a maintenance alcoholic for fourteen years or so. During the day, I used beer and shots for that utilitarian buzz. At cocktail parties, I was a standard drunk. The cocaine, though, seemed to increase my capacity. While I wasn't falling down all the time, I did sleep a lot on the floor.

I began to restrict my drinking to keep it manageable. I drank in the kitchen where the bottles were. I went through a series of personalities and tried them on like new suits. Finally, when I was forty, I couldn't find any more role models. Maybe I was a failure.

I was less and less able to escape. The places where I could briefly escape were no longer the Starlite Club or my room with the R & B in the dark or the road to the woods with Susie, the blond girl. The places now were just blank and empty hells. Small-time hells.

I was right at the doorway to the real thing, but I couldn't describe it. I called a woman I knew who'd been sober for six years or so. She took me to my first AA meeting, where I found a whole new bunch of people to imitate, at least until I didn't need to anymore.

I was a tough case. They were trying to separate me from my best friend, my only friend, really. I struggled. Then one afternoon I was at an AA birthday party with 150 people. We were all broken up into groups and activities and meetings, and I suddenly looked around and saw how good everything was. I suddenly saw.

I guess I could have seen anytime, but I had all this stuff I carried around that had come to seem important.

I didn't have to wear my hair like Ricky. I didn't have to draw cartoons to amuse others, and I didn't have to be hip, slick, and cool. That was wonderful, though maybe I was still kind of empty.

I embraced the program because it offered me everything I wanted: relaxed friendship and freedom from alcohol. I wasn't a slave anymore. I believed. I accepted God and came to believe. I was all right, though still kind of empty and scared sometimes, like it was all another place I'd made out of nothing. Something was still missing, you know?

I believed in the God in the Steps, but I can't say that I had an experience of God beyond the good that had come to me in the wake of not drinking. That was a lot! But I had a haunting feeling of dumb luck about everything.

It was in 1995 that I went back to my family. I had memories there. *Family* was suddenly a slightly different word; it contained power. I met a wonderful woman and married her. We each had two children when we got married.

I was becoming comfortable with saying, "I wouldn't be here but by the grace of God." I was blessed, and sometimes I knew it. I didn't really know that being blessed could mean something beyond things going well, or that there was a deeper contact to be made with God that had nothing to do with well-being, a predictable life, or even happiness.

I found out.

Right now, this afternoon, my son is dead and my life is revolving around that fact like one of those old paper birds on string we had when we were kids. That's heartbreaking to say— "when we were kids."

There was a funeral. There were memorials and trips. I still can't work or think effectively. I write and read too much e-mail.

I feel myself getting lost in the grief and becoming isolated. I worry about my marriage. I write to senators, a thankless task. I read too many articles on Latin American revolutionaries and their enemies, on nepotistic cover-ups, on bananas, on coffee, on cocaine, on substitution crops, on flowers, on gold. I try to figure out what to do, what I should be doing.

I listen to the politicians talking about American interests and understand that for every atrocity committed, a whole new generation of idealists will spring up in opposition, nonviolent or warlike. There's comfort in that, but not much. My son had a good heart. He went there to help, and they killed him. The events are still a mystery, the events are brutal. The international outcry over the oil companies and the exploitation continues. More kids get killed.

Terry's brother is a musician in New York. He's fine, but now his life has a terrible fragility to me. I worry all the time. I try new hobbies and throw them away. I try to write. I work at finding peace.

(I know working at it doesn't work, but I have to.)

Terry spent his time helping other people. I'd like to do that. He was always away somewhere, but when he'd come back, we were as close as ever. When he was a teenager, he even helped me with my sobriety. He accomplished a lot.

Everything I think and feel is a little disjointed. Memories and images follow each other without any logic except for the terrible organizing principle that Terry is dead.

When I was drinking and using, I was one of those drunks who excused himself by saying, "At least I'm a good father. I may be a failure, but at least I'm a good father." I used my kids until Terry was dead. I guess I could have kept going, but I didn't. I could have talked up his virtues and my contribution to his virtues, but I stopped. Once you see what you're doing, it's hard to keep doing it—unless you're going to drink again. The wire services published a smiling photo of him I'd taken myself.

I miss him so. I hardly know what to do.

I've begun to understand what keeps me from despair. It isn't any sense of well-being, comfort, and day-to-day predictability. How could it be?

I was driving down 101 toward the Golden Gate one morning,

not too long after I got the news of my son's death. Then I was in prison in my head. The Starlite is gone from the cliff face now, and has been for many years, but I noticed it not being there just like I always do. I can't remember where I was going that morning. It doesn't matter.

As I took the big turn down to the bridge, I suddenly felt the overpowering presence of God. It was all in the one moment. Everything was suddenly so beautiful that I couldn't stand it. It was as if I'd been allowed to see things as they are for the first time. It just overwhelmed me. I was so happy.

Whether or not the day-to-day pain went away (it didn't), it didn't matter anymore because I'd been allowed to see the way things really are, and there wasn't any possible response other than joy. Anything else would have been a step down the ladder, and a lie.

It was like I suddenly wasn't myself—I was who I really am. The gratitude I felt was overwhelming. I still am myself, most of the time, however miserable I get, and the certainty, the odd happiness, comes over me suddenly without healing or changing anything.

It isn't that I feel that I'm special to God or special in general. It's just that I know I have the strength to get through this with nothing but a broken heart and everything beautiful around me.

I'm completely grateful, however strange that might sound. Gratitude is all I need. It's all I want for myself.

CHAPTER FIVE

The Dead Talking

THE DAY AFTER Peter finished this interview, his doctor told him he had four days to live. He'd been sick for a long time, but wanted very much to finish this, to get it done, finally—as if there were something his life had to say and he had to get it right. His voice was frail and sometimes difficult to listen to, because he wanted it to be able to do more than it could. His pain and frustration showed.

It wasn't that he thought of himself, or his death, in a special light. It wasn't even that he felt the need to leave something behind so people would know he'd been here. He was passing on information because he knew it to be important to the mass of people who'd continue living without him. He wasn't sure if he could say what the information was, but it made no difference to the need to pass it on. In that sense the effort, and the sounds he finally made, had much to do with poetry, as do all these voices.

There's a substance to be communicated, though the mind and the tongue aren't always quite up to it. Still, the effort itself, the voice on its own, in pure intent, is surpassingly intense and beautiful. Which is why I keep saying, "Listen carefully." The voices say what can't be said, and sometimes the points of grace are scattered, like pieces of light in the grass, in the air, in the cloud—with nothing but a broken heart and everything beautiful around me.

So Peter is dead now. What does that mean? Not much. The landscape is littered with dead people, and a lot of them are still talking. The largest part of everything ever written is dead people talking. We come in at one end and leave at the other, and if we're lucky, we leave a presence or voice behind. When it addresses the human crisis, that's as good as it gets.

There are dead people who are more real to me than many alive. There are dead people who live in me. Their voices exist in the air as one and many at the same time. They're saying, "Pay attention: there's one thing to be said. And after it's said, it has to be felt in the whole body, like the breath."

I'm at the age when friends start to die, three in the last two years. I can't say it's depressing because it really isn't. I can't even say they leave holes in my life, because they don't. I miss them, and sometimes I find myself thinking they're still alive. I think I'll call, but then remember, "Oh, yeah, Susan's not here anymore." But those are little things at best, and death is a very large thing. I hear Susan in my head—we were together for a long time and she's always there—and my friend Richard who sometimes seems to be riding with me in the car he gave me before he died. I hear him saying, "You know, it's like there's a lot of us think we're too intelligent to say 'God.'"

Maybe the unborn are with us, too, just harder to hear because there's no frame of reference, there are no memories.

The voices say the same things, and they have been since there were voices.

There's beauty here. God, how lovely it is, and how lovely it could make us if we'd stop for a bit, look, and understand the perfectly un-understandable being of God, his loveliness.

In a bookstore the other day I picked up a coffee table book, *The Art of the Ice Age*, and flipped through it absentmindedly. I had to return to a page that had flapped by in a fraction of a second.

It was a simple thick outline of a mastodon. Inside it, a heart had been drawn, a valentine heart, right where the mastodon's heart would have been. I stared at it for a bit and tried to understand, but there wasn't anything to understand. The eye of the human had honored the beast with a drawing of his being, and went further to his secret interior. He'd extended himself into the mastodon, the other, and granted him grace and his own consciousness.

It seemed to me that the connection between them was God and that the universe is nothing but points of contact vibrating—heard and unheard, seen and unseen.

Death makes space, so things don't clog and run down. Particles jump, comets stream, living things die, and the sudden open space is filled at the far end, so the movement in time is continuous.

Peter was a sweet man with a boyish voice, wavering sometimes, cracking with effort, but he didn't see his death as special either and moved on, I think, right into the stream of voices all saying that same thing, "Pay attention, the moments pass and each is filled with meaning."

He was in a lot of pain. Sometimes he'd pause, wait, and then look around for the sentence he'd been in before the pain hit and took his breath away.

What I hear in Pete is the edge of a consciousness that

something unusual was going on through all his life. While it made no sense, it was almost as if his life had been commenting on itself, somehow, and with odd voices saying things like, "Why don't you build a church instead?" Instead of a prison.

Looking back, bits of grace appear in unlikely places—never, almost never, in the trappings of religiosity and conventional sanctity. Just little bits of light and odd phrases make moments that stay in the mind so you have to go back every once in a while and think, "What was that?"

It doesn't matter what you tell yourself. It doesn't matter that you wanted to be what you've become. There's still a voice murmuring to itself. Before you wanted to be what you've become, someone else, who was a pretty good kid, wanted something different.

Pete knew that his strength came from the heart of the world, not from the reality outside, where his son has been killed for doing good, and knew that the center of meaning is all good and all love.

He wanted to stay in that place where he could pump the swing high and see over the fence to the trees of the shadowy lane where the little girl walked. We all do that. Maybe there's a way to slow this down, we think, and we try to stay in the places where the fright and pain aren't.

The kid who knows early on that nothing stays, nothing is solid, is in a bad place. "Oh God, let me slow it down," the kid might pray, but then asks, "What God? Nothing stays so I'll make my own safe places."

It feels like alcohol or drugs might do it, but the real slowing, when it comes, is in how you see and feel. The more you let in, the longer the seeing takes.

"I wish I could be there again, and a child, and Mommy

singing in the blue light with the music, and the Bay, and the safety of the light." I have those places, too. Everyone has those places, however thin, however flawed. Bits of light are strewn through lives, embedded in brains and waiting for a recognition, a sudden piece of the whole perception that makes the points vibrate and flare. A whole being alive, at once, so that whatever is immediate is real in a new way, edged in light, radiant.

Have you ever heard anyone offer a coherent explanation of the evolutionary role of the aesthetic sense? I mean they worry all the time about altruism and how a being caught up in the great chains of survival could possibly do something that doesn't serve it. The answer of course is, "Well, they do. So start from there, hotshot."

What about beauty? Has there ever been a civilization that didn't recognize the beauty of the sky and didn't respond to the immensity of light and color?

Why? Or what's to be gained?

Four years ago when I was leaving the house early with my one-year-old son on my shoulder, he turned his head to the sun rising down at the end of the street, and smiled in absolute joy.

What did he see?

What did Peter see dying in a room with bedclothes and light through the blinds and things arranged in space with colors and outlines, water in a glass shining, shadows angling down and up and fading into the flatness, bright eyes in faces, everything built around him with hallways running away, and closed places out there with towels and linens, cans and bottles, rooms with light in them, curtains moving in breezes, plants breathing and stirring?

He was in enormous pain. Still, he took the time to do this interview because he wanted to tell us that through the physical pain and the overwhelming grief and certainty of extinction he saw God, lovely and everywhere.

Peter died on the twenty-ninth of July, 2002. He remains in loving memory.

❧

The next voice is my own.

CHAPTER SIX

Larry

I WAS BORN in Brooklyn in 1943. I remember a lot, back to when I was two, maybe one.

My father was Irish from Galway, and my mother was a Scot from Glasgow. They had both been in the country for a while, so their accents were soft and musical. The sounds of the voices were quite lovely, though my mother could be shrill. When she screamed, it was hard to get away.

We lived in a big apartment building on Eighty-sixth in Bay Ridge. Bay Ridge is just off the Narrows, where the harbor thins before it opens out into the Atlantic. My father and I walked down there a lot on Sunday mornings.

One day, while standing at the front of the ferry across the Narrows to Staten Island, it seemed like I understood everything, but I didn't know what it was I understood. We were on the thin top edge of all this water and right underneath was more water, and who knew what was there? I didn't think I could tell anybody that.

On my father's side, I came from melancholy Irishmen. My father never said anything about his father's drinking, but years later my aunt Elizabeth told me, "The family has always had trouble with the drink." She was a hundred years old then and in a Franciscan nursing home. She'd never had problems with it. She'd been upright, formal, and deeply pious. She'd fight with my father about his working on Sunday. He was a machinist, and he worked alone.

My mother's family lived right across the street from us. Her sister Meg and Jimmy, Meg's husband, and Ronnie and Norma, twins who were four years older than me, and John, who was four years older than them. John was a paratrooper in Korea—a big man I barely knew. On my mother's side, we were almost all redheads. My father had red hair when he was a boy, but he was forty-two when I was born. My mother was thirty-two.

The Scots all drank, and there was a wild unpredictability to their lives. Jimmy would go missing and turn up in the hospital, rolled for his paycheck. Men would come to the door to take the furniture away.

There was a long back alley with gardens behind Aunt Meg's house. I'd be sent out there to play when my mother was working at the shop. I was scared to go out there, down the stairs to all those strange kids. I asked my father what to do (I was still able to do that), and he said, "Just say 'Boo!' Surprise them." I knew it wouldn't work, but I tried it anyway. It didn't work.

Ronnie and Norma took care of me, sort of, when my mother was away. I liked them fine. They both died in the same year, 1993, of alcoholism. I had a hard time finding that out because the family doesn't keep in touch. When my mother died, Norma called to tell me and to say I didn't have to come. Mother had been cremated and everything was taken care of. Norma knew I was in bad shape then, so she just took care of it. I don't know where my mother's or my father's ashes went. There's nobody left who could tell me.

Of my mother's five brothers and sisters, three died from alcohol. Lily, who'd been a saint, my mother always said, had died of something else. Willie had been a drunk and froze to death in the street on Third Avenue. I always hated Third Avenue. At our end of the street were bars, and at the other end was Bush Terminal and tenements and my father's machine shop. I was afraid of being poor. We were working class and money was a problem, though Aunt Elizabeth gave herself airs. My mother fretted about money a lot and sang sad songs.

My mother and father read books, were generally soft-spoken, and they didn't at all share in the local politics. At every other AA meeting, you'll hear, "I always felt different. I always wanted to be like the others." Well, we were a little different.

My father didn't drink much. My mother drank more, with her sister, but not every day. Later, when they were older and sick, and things were going to hell, they both drank a lot. My mother died when she fell down drunk and hit her head. It may have been a stroke, Norma said.

Willie was the designated drunk in the family. My mother always talked about him with love, but she told me that if he came to the door while I was alone in the house, I wasn't to let him in. It happened only once when I was about ten. I've never forgotten. He was in a long brown overcoat, his eyes were help-less, and I kept looking past him at the wall. He only wanted a shower and a cup of tea. He always called me Lawrence. I think he gradually became like a Christ in my head. He was com-pletely helpless; all he had was pain. The moment of seeing it has stayed with me always.

I grew up by retreating. I was sure my father—who to me was a kindly and loving God and a secret judge at the same time—never felt I was living up to his expectations. He never told me that, but I thought he was afraid I was too much like my mother.

I was afraid that my mother was going to follow up on her threats to leave him and take me with her. "Don't say a word," she'd say. "Now don't be saying a word."

I turned into a spy and a traitor. I had dark failings like my mother. My father was afraid of them. I had information I wasn't giving him, and it ate me up. He'd take me out every Sunday to wonderful places, and I'd hold his hand somberly. "Smile, darn you. Smile," he'd sometimes say good-naturedly.

My mother told me one morning that I'd had a sister, but she'd died. She was a little girl, with red hair too, and she died when we were born. I've run the memory through my head compulsively. It was a Saturday morning right after *Big Jon and Sparky* on the radio, and she'd been doing the dishes while I listened. The little radio was in the kitchen. She had been singing "Mary, Mary, long before the fashions changed . . ." Out of nowhere, she told me about my sister who had died at birth. Nobody else ever mentioned it.

When I asked my aunt years later in the nursing home, she looked confused and said, "No, I don't remember that." Then she added, "She only lived for half an hour."

When I look at the early pictures, I'm never with my mother. It's always Elizabeth, my cousin Bill, or Lynn, his daughter. But never my mother. So I begin to wonder where she was and how she was with me.

As I said, the notion of God became an embarrassment to me, though I wished a lot that we went to church, any church, because every other kid in the building did. I'd lie to them and say I went to Saint Patrick's, way down Fourth. Saint Anselm's, three blocks away, was the local church.

The stories in the Brothers Grimm that I read and reread were confusing about God. There was one in which a little girl opens a door in heaven and sees the Trinity sitting in flames. I had no idea what that meant. When I was ten or so I started reading the Old Testament, but it pretty much bored me. Over the years, I limited myself to looking up things that interested me. I remember wanting to know about the Tower of Babel, because the image stirred something in me.

My overall impression was that the God in the Old Testament wasn't very nice. There seemed to be no reason to care about him except for the fact that he'd knock you down if you didn't.

I used to try to find out if he existed by tempting him. I'd run in the street and say to myself, "If I can't get home without stepping on a line, then God is shit." He never struck me down. I saw him with the standard white beard and sandals, and I think I worried about hell, but not as a full-time resident.

So I got more and more alone in my head, and I learned some ways of protecting myself.

One Halloween I went with some of the kids to a Lutheran church down on Ridge Boulevard. We were going to collect money for UNICEF. There was a dance afterward, with music and orange lights. I was very happy and felt like I belonged there. I met a girl named Laura there, too, and I liked her a lot. I thought that maybe I needed to be in the church, but I had to seriously consider it. Besides, my going to church would have pained my father.

Years later, when I hadn't been sober for long, humiliation and fear would wash over me. I trained myself to think about that church basement whenever I felt the pain and the fear. It worked pretty well, as if I set up a switch in my head that I could flick and turn off the pain.

I got started drinking when I went home from school for

lunch one afternoon. I didn't go back to school because I was too embarrassed. Someone I'd thought was my friend had humiliated me in front of the class. He had told the girl about my feelings toward her. So after lunch at home, I had a couple of shots of port out of the bottle under the kitchen cabinet. It tasted good and calmed me.

My mother wasn't saying much about leaving my dad anymore. She'd still get hysterical, though, and I'd hold my breath before dinner, hoping they wouldn't get in a fight. I often sided with my father, but I felt like I was betraying him because I knew stuff I'd never told him.

Sometimes I'd be outside at night, when the air was cool, and I'd get taken to another place like heaven. The stars were so beautiful. I'd run as fast as I could, as if I could run off the planet.

My general approach to the world was to put one foot in front of the other and try not to let them take me by surprise. My ecstatic world was a secret. I was a drunk waiting to happen; and I was a deeply spiritual child without a clue.

So, the drinking. Sometimes I'd take a swig out of the scotch bottle. The afternoon I had a terrible sore throat my mother gave me a big glass of scotch, hot water, honey, and lemon. I got quite drunk, lying on the couch and watching television. It was a sort of exalted feeling, as if it were suddenly possible for me to be at home in the world. It was like being God.

All through my childhood (longer than that, I guess), I found myself predicting disasters and trying to imagine how I would remedy them. I often thought about what would happen if my mother or father died. I tried to figure out which would be better. I tried to think coldly, so I wouldn't have to feel that I was wishing anyone dead. I thought that when I finally got away from the apartment, things would be all right.

Gradually I got to be a bright kid who looked on religion as a sign of stupidity. Organized religion as such means very little to me, unless it's voices in a group, praying or singing.

On the other hand, I had always understood, I can't say how, that stupidity was nothing to look down on. Actually, I do know where I got that—my parents were intensely decent people and taught it to me. So I knew that the fact that I was able to read a lot of books didn't make me any better than the kid who was born an athlete. Secretly, probably, I would rather have been the athlete.

My father had a kind of melancholy feud with the church. When movies were religious, with a lot of sentiment, I'd squirm in my seat and get deeply embarrassed. I knew he disapproved, and it always seemed to me that if there was something wrong in a movie, it was my fault. Somehow, it was an embarrassment for him to know I was hearing it, and that embarrassed me. It was nuts.

My father had been an altar boy in Galway, and his mother had caught pneumonia and died after making some pilgrimage, climbing a hill in the rain on her knees to kiss a priest's ring. She'd come home and died. My father and his three sisters had been split up among relatives. Not one of them went by the names they'd been born with.

I had information I wasn't giving him, and it ate me up. He'd take me out every Sunday, to wonderful places, and I'd hold his hand somberly. We were odd, I thought, and different. I thought we were crazy. Later I understood that everyone was crazy, and only the ones who couldn't hide successfully got caught.

I got more and more alone in my head, and I learned some ways of protecting myself. I spoke to some kids from my building last year and they said that I had seemed to be amused at everything and lofty.

I would have preferred to be any number of other people— Leo Durocher, Robert Louis Stevenson, Walt Disney, Donald O'Connor, Don Mueller, Dean Stockwell, Edward R. Murrow— but I wasn't willing to take instruction. Or maybe I was willing but just couldn't bring it off. There's a book called *The Autobiography of a Schizophrenic Girl* by Marguerite Sechehaye; in it she says, "Fear made me ill." It's a perfect truth—fear makes you ill.

I don't know how I got scared. I always felt alone, I guess, and I never believed anything I was told. Why is that? I don't know. I tried to believe what my father told me, and most of it turned out to be true, but some part in my head kept saying, "Nobody knows." That's true, of course, but I feared that I'd get trapped and not be able to slip away, to do whatever I wanted to do. To say no. Whatever it was, it was a terrific foundation for loneliness and madness.

When I was eleven, everything (everything fearful) came together in a dream and unhinged me so badly that, I believe now, I was mad for six months or more. I couldn't do anything but feel the dream and know it was waiting for me again. I'd see twilight come and my spine would get tense. I'd try to think of things I liked, things I might be able to do before it was night, but they left me alone in the dark again.

In the dream my parents and I were in a kind of gallery in a basement. Some men were carrying a coffin to a furnace in the wall, to push it in. My father said, "He was a traitor." My mother said, "That's horrible," and I woke up knowing I'd never sleep again without fear.

It faded slowly through the winter. I'd hear songs in school choir like "The Skater's Waltz," "Ciribiribin," and "Oh, My Papa," and when I hear them now I get just a little stab of what it was like.

Coming home in the bleak afternoons, I'd want to drink the port, but I couldn't because the level had already gone down a bit. I didn't think about suicide, but I thought about dying. Everything kept moving.

I barely remember junior high school except for endless embarrassments and the big old copy of *Moby Dick* that I read through the library periods. I learned a great deal reading it. Not just from the narrative, but from the way the narrative moved, and the way the voice changed all the time. And the sudden visions—the whales in the glassy water. I liked Ahab's defiance, too, though he was stupid about it, too much out in the open.

In junior high school, I waited for high school and loathed myself for my cowardice with girls. I couldn't make the gesture, reaching out and touching. I just couldn't do it, though there were any number of girls who were willing. I was in love with Carol, in my building, and she was right there, willing, and I couldn't touch her. I was a mess. I'd stay that way till I got out of high school and went away to college to get seriously drunk with a warm sense of "at last."

So from 1959 to 1981, I was more or less drunk. The things I did were enormously sad, pointless, and vicious, but nothing out of the ordinary for humanity. That's the funny thing. In a group, you spend three days getting a guy to talk about some terrible secret, and when he finally does, it's something common not only to the drunks in the room but to human beings generally.

I drank my way through school and did nothing at all for

myself. I met the woman I'd marry, who was perfectly lovely, and took her away from her family to a place she didn't want to be, San Francisco, with people she didn't particularly like.

There's a betrayal involved in my talking about those years, and I don't want to do it. As Robert Creeley wrote, "My love's manners in bed are not to be discussed by me"—nor is anything else, in loving memory.

We had a son in 1965. We were too young to handle it. When we came home from the hospital with Brandan, Susan was holding him, and I went into the bathroom. When I came out, she was sitting on the floor, holding him, and crying helplessly because she didn't know what to do or how to take care of an infant. So I pretended *I* knew.

I decided almost consciously that all I had to do was keep the edge off, the fear, with alcohol. Then I'd be able to take care of my family and no one would know how I was doing it. I'd be just like everyone else and well respected. I wanted those things. They were in my head like an Eden. I knew they weren't real and that what I really wanted was to be, I don't know, offhandedly capable and decent like my father. But I knew I never would be, because I was a secret and a traitor and too weak for the world.

I tried to explain to my father. The year before he died he came out to California, and we were sitting one night, drinking. I played some records for him I knew he'd never heard. I thought maybe I could talk around them, explain, make some sense, tell him I loved him. I could explain that all the misery had just been the way I was, the way I was born, and that I didn't blame anyone for anything. I wanted to tell him that I loved him and ask if he'd please understand and please look at me as if I weren't a disappointment.

The only two songs I remember are John Lennon's "Mother

(Daddy, come home!)" and Rod Stewart's "Dirty Old Town (and we'll chop you down!)." I told him clearly what I wanted. And it was the truth. Nothing ever came of it, because when you're drunk you can say whatever the fuck you want to say and it doesn't mean a thing. The next morning began the way all the others had. Nothing had changed. Nothing ever changes in Alcoholville.

We lived on the coast north of San Francisco in a town called Bolinas, population about five hundred, thirty of them writers. I'd published a book that did pretty well, and we'd bought a house. "At last," I'd thought, "my son is safe and we can all just relax and everything will be fine. This is a small town, not like Brooklyn. Small school, easygoing." The one book had done well, but I went back to poetry exclusively, and there was no money in that.

There was a gap in my head between what was really going on and what I wanted to go on, between the person I really was or seemed to be and the person I wanted to be, between the love I felt at three in the morning, drinking in the dark, and the love I couldn't live up to day to day. It was all an endless desert between who I'd wanted to be and who I was. My one, very personal achievement was that nobody knew who I was.

If the school was pretty bad for Brandan, if he came home crying, then I'd have to sit with him and try to explain what to do to get himself out of his misery and aloneness. I did not have a clue, just like my father. There was a point where the alcohol broke off my pain and I could say, "Wait till the morning. It will be better."

It was sad and wretched, and even today I can't see it happening any differently. My son is a wonderful man married to a wonderful woman. But I still see the pain and the demons around him and hear my own voice trying to be measured and calm but lying, because when the calmness was over there'd be incoherence and chaos and a little boy's hopes violated.

My wife got sadder and sadder and started to believe in power and marijuana, quietly taking the power in the house to herself as I threw it off and settled into nothing but avoidance.

Not so oddly, I found myself in the middle of the night writing poems that began, "I keep waiting for God to talk to me," or "The world is not in my head. Is not. The world is not in my head."

I became obsessed with the notion of God at a distance. I didn't believe, but I was a Manichaean of sorts. I had a sense of evil as an isolated place, infinitely far from God. My head was a desert, but at least I was trying to get across (one foot in front of the other). I didn't even know what "God" meant. I used the word like a corkscrew, to try to get myself open.

Around me, my wife's anguish was huge, and my son was watching everything fall apart. All I'd wanted was to be consistent for him and not to bring hysteria into his life. Yet his early childhood had been spent moving from doubtful place to doubtful place, and now I'd settled him into a house he couldn't escape.

When I bought him a bike he was suddenly gone for long periods. I didn't mind. It seemed to me that while he was out in the air, on his bike, I couldn't hurt him. I went deeper into my own head and forgot he had his own soul and wasn't me, and couldn't be understood as me.

When an acid-casualty psychotic burned our house down, we had to live in another place and rebuild first. The work was enormous, because I'd never built a house before. I brooded and thought about it day and night, and stayed drunk so I wouldn't have to feel.

But you feel anyway. My controlling image was of God receding in space, a redshift I saw in the night sky while I was lying in the backyard of our new place, waiting for the guy who burned the house down to come around. I had a camp light, a shotgun, a bottle of vodka, and a copy of Eliot's *Four Quartets,* which was somehow the source of the redshifted God.

God wasn't retreating, I was. But it was hard to tell the difference.

We didn't have enough insurance money to finish the house. Things got very bad indeed. My wife asked me to leave, and I said, "Fine. I'll go to New York where I can get work, and I'll send you money."

I would have given my life to make things different. I just couldn't find it or anyone who wanted it. That's how it felt, anyway. I considered a monastery, but wouldn't have known how to begin. The world was blocked. I was going to die, and I figured it would be nice if at least I could contract something fatal and take to my bed with some dignity left.

I can't say I was full of self-pity. I pretty much knew what had happened and knew I'd done it. I was full of hope, if anything. I just didn't recognize it for what it was. I thought it was despair. I was a battered house with a room in it that couldn't really be there because there wasn't any space for it. The walls and the spaces were all accounted for. When I was a teenager, I'd dream of my old elementary school, and there'd be a secret center to it I could never find, a place of unbearable mystery and sweetness, like the mind's womb—a room full of clouds, shadowy and sweet. I knew it was there, I just couldn't find it.

I don't mean some out-of-the-world place where there's no pain and everything is just wonderful. The world is never that, not if you're sane or honest. I still can't handle the moments of feeling the range of what's going on in the world at any particular moment. There's a particularly American notion of enlightenment as a spiritual one-upmanship that I loathe.

But there is a place you can reach sometimes, when you need to, where future, past, and present make sense and you feel a willingness to give yourself up. Not give somebody else up, but give yourself up. In that place, I can say, "Whatever happens, the good is still everything." To me, the good means God.

Talking, talking. Talking was part of my problem, because no matter how broken and crazed I got, I could always seem reasonable and articulate so that when I was screaming for help my voice was coming out measured, in sentences. The words were killing me and I couldn't stop. Talking was part of the guy I'd made up when I was five, and I couldn't let him go. Sometimes, like when I went to the Long Island University extension hospital in Brooklyn, all they had to do was look at me, and they'd fetch a wheelchair and put me to sleep.

At times, when you're walking in the street, a little incident comes up, like an old embarrassment. It has the whole weight of your life attached to it. You feel compelled to get away as fast as you can and start talking out loud, saying anything at all, just so the words pull the mind back.

I was walking on upper Broadway. God knows what I said, but I suddenly saw myself saying it because the woman coming toward me was looking at me like you look at one of those people you see on Broadway who talk to themselves. Behind her, there was a guy who was shambling, crazed, with enormous pain. We looked at each other going by like we were the only two in the street who could see, if you know what I mean.

All I had in New York was being. I was there. I could walk, even if I had to be careful and stand back from the subways coming into the station because I was seizing a lot. I was lucky, really, because I'd come to the place where the alcohol doesn't work anymore and you can see yourself clearly as a fleshly thing with a made-up personality.

In the hospital, I played whist with a woman with a terrible scar and a man who'd tried to kill his family with an ax while he was drunk. It was just time out of time, and affected me very little. I charmed the doctor in charge, and he gave me the address of a writer's AA meeting in Gramercy Park. I was never going to go, but I talked it up.

It all blurs. Moments of clarity in those days helped, but they didn't stop me. It was as if something tugged at my sleeve and said, "Look at this," and I did, and went on. I kept going for another seven months.

Back in California, I tried to kill myself a couple of times. I remember lying all night on Mount Tamalpais after I had cut my wrists and passed out, then woke up and cut my ankles and put them in the stream. I then passed out again and woke up. The sun was coming up, and I was just about dead. I could feel it. All I had to do was let my mind slide away.

I thought about my son, who was twelve, and exactly what my suicide would do to him, and then crawled slowly, agonizingly, across a little meadow to a hiking trail. A jogger found me. It was a piece of grace that brought my son to my mind.

Through all of it, I was intensely conscious of the beautiful. The stone walls at Central Park were beautiful, and I knew

Belvedere Tower was, but I couldn't get there. The air was very bright. The face on the Chinese waiter on Broadway who brought me soup was lovely.

On the mountain, I'd been in a glade of forget-me-nots by a stream, and the sun came down on them so they were dappled and thick. Everything around was beautiful except that I was stuck inside myself and there was nothing there but more time with nothing in it. I was kind of a clock-watcher.

There wasn't one single moment, but a series of them. Look at this, pause; look at this, pause. The one that really stands out is a morning I was trying to get across Broadway to have my soup and buy a bottle. Snow piled on the ground and the street, up around Ninety-fifth, with the island in the middle. My feet were just about not working. I looked at them, trying to hold it together. I said to myself, "You're still alive and you don't know. You're still alive and you don't know. One foot in front of the other. What might happen. What might happen."

I was moving so carefully I got scared trying to cross from the island to the other side. The light changed while I was in the middle. I turned and saw the cars coming at me. I remember the shine of the green one. I couldn't have been seeing the real car because it was old, perhaps a '47 Plymouth.

In California, I sat at the edge of Bolinas Lagoon, and the hills across the way were moving down into the water in colored snakes. That was beautiful too, but I hurt so much I couldn't be in my head.

The beautiful *was* God for me, but I didn't know it then. I believed that I didn't deserve a God and that there was some dignity to be salvaged from brooding on his absence. It wasn't that God didn't exist. No, it was that I'd taken him into my closed system—my old notion of God was helping me stay drunk. But the beauty of things was tugging at my sleeve.

I keep coming back to that walk across Broadway because it was everything. Then a clarity existed that I could almost breathe. It was the pure truth, and I told it to myself. "You don't know." I think I gave up right then, and the rest was just the winding down. Some machines take a long time to shut off.

It's a sacred place for me—halfway across Broadway at Ninety-fifth with one foot back and one clumsily in the air. God didn't talk to me, I did. Then everything that was God came flooding in. I wanted to cry but couldn't, so I went to the liquor store and got a half pint of hundred proof and took it with me in my pocket to the Chinese restaurant.

The only other thing from then that I remember in the same way is the woman on the Seventh Avenue IRT. She gave me her seat in the rush hour. I was running from imaginary assassins and had cracked ribs from a seizure, and I was hanging on to the strap. "Here," she said. "You look ill. Sit down." I thanked her and sat there staring into her thighs and belly. I was astonished and wanted to cry but couldn't. I'd already been exposed.

Finally, I just gave up. I'd been sleeping on a friend's floor and "The Tennessee Waltz" had been going around in my head. I'd pissed on myself, and I woke up as the sun was coming up. I sat outside in the garden, then later made my way downtown (it took a long time). I tried to call the people at this treatment house I'd applied to and then run away from. But I couldn't get my finger in the holes of the pay phone and had to go into the grocery store and talk the guy behind the counter into letting me have a bottle of sweet wine. He was very kind. I drank it in back of the store, then went back to the phone with my fingers steady.

That was the last drink I had.

In treatment, I looked at the blue veins in my arms in the shower and figured how I'd cut them if I had to. I said, "You don't know" to myself, over and over. "Put one foot in front of the other," I'd remind myself. Gradually it didn't matter anymore that my clanking personality required all this stuff to feed it. I was just where I was. I was so grateful, and so afraid that the street was still out there.

The only prayer I had was "Please help me." I think now that my life consisted of trying as hard as I could. It wasn't enough, but I did try very hard, and without the alcohol maybe it could have been different. I understand that God made himself available at every point, at every juncture, but God had no power, only a loveliness everywhere waiting to be touched.

I have no God who thinks and acts like a powerful human being. I didn't have that God when I was a child, and I don't now. There's a love that is not an emotion and a gratitude that's all love and not attached to anything at all. I wish I could pass it on, but I can't, except to the degree that I can make myself a transfer point.

Gratitude is a substance that doesn't diminish but grows when it's given away. You take and you give and the world comes around. God doesn't need praise or fancy clothes or translators. God needs to be touched and passed along, and not like money.

I think of my parents and it hurts. I think about my dead wife and the misery of my son, and that hurts. I think about what I did through everything—all the humiliations, avoidances, and cruelties—and that hurts my vanity. I shudder at my own shallowness.

But sometimes I walk out in the air and human beings are so beautiful in their effort that I'm really astounded. I think, "God, how hard we try."

It's easier to touch love and be grateful. In my life, it started in little things and stayed in little things, but that means nothing anyway. Lives are short, and everything in them has equal weight. Like when we're dying and it's okay, finally, if we let it be.

Everything I have is in the One. You don't know what will happen. Stay alive. Everything is just waking up. Look around.

CHAPTER SEVEN

Like a Gyroscope

THAT WAS MY OWN VOICE, and I don't have a lot more to say.

I was sitting in my workroom. It has bookshelves, pictures on the wall, and a wide window with venetian blinds behind a dark wood desk.

I'm pretty much bald on top, with thicker whitened hair swept back at the sides. I wear glasses, and you can tell my hair was once red from the backs of my hands. I move my glasses back and forth on the nose as I speak.

I have a movie poster on the right wall—*Moonrise*, 1948. Gail Russell is comforting Dane Clark. Ethel Barrymore is a disembodied head at the bottom. My desk chair swivels. I'm fifty-nine.

Human beings are so much alike that the differences between anyone, people like Saint Francis, Dick Cheney, and Ethel Merman, are small, except in terms of effect. All the time the soul is sitting in the back of the head like a gyroscope, waiting to be noticed.

God is waiting to be noticed. One can be lonely and touched by God. One can be mad and touched by God. God is available.

Maybe I could have known that if the world had been that way when I was a child. Or if people had talked to children that way.

❧

The next voice is Matt's. In many positive ways, he's still a child, waiting for someone to talk to him. Some voices just hurt. Matt is here not because he had a sudden bright insight or a dramatic fall into grace, but because he's a voice from a very lonely place. His uneloquent recognitions are perfectly styled to that place and perfectly workable for him.

He's at a school for troubled teenagers. It's late afternoon and we've met in the library, which is also the principal's office. We sit at an ordinary library table, and the sun is filtered through trees and the long, horizontal blinds.

Matt is sixteen and has a face in a Leonardo DiCaprio mold. Not quite as self-conscious, perhaps. Not self-conscious at all, really, as if he'd looked at himself for a long time through other people's eyes and found little of interest. Matt is deeply troubling. I think he should be disturbing to everyone who still thinks or feels underneath the flat surface of our rationalized inattention.

CHAPTER EIGHT

Matt

I'LL TELL YOU A LITTLE about my background. I grew up in a pretty normal family, not poor and not really rich. Both my parents were abnormal drinkers. It was my mom, dad, a little brother, and me.

I grew up sipping off my dad's beers. I always felt attracted to alcohol. It was like pretty normal stuff, you know. I played baseball, sports. My dad was a firefighter and my mom was a housewife. I grew up in a pretty normal place in Tiburon, California. I went to Reed School, Bel Air, third through sixth grade when I started drinking. Yeah.

When I got a little older, maybe in the fourth grade, I was really more attracted to drugs and alcohol. I dunno. I was attracted to something. That lifestyle of the older kids—I was just attracted to it. I thought it was cool. I wanted to *be* them.

So I started drinking. In sixth grade, with the first drink I took, I really set out to get drunk. I was twelve years old then, and I had a friend whose parents owned the property where this concert was being held. They had a cabin there, and that's where I had the first drink I took to get drunk. It felt good. I felt warm inside. Sierra Nevada Pale Ale.

I smoked marijuana that weekend, too. I coughed a lot but then, the beer soothed that. And I liked it right from then. I thought it was the best thing that had ever happened to me.

So I took a bunch of marijuana home and I started, y'know, taking beer from my dad and smoking marijuana. It was just great. I would tell my mom I was gonna go down to the local swimming pool, and we'd hook up, drink, and smoke marijuana. It was great for a while, but then Dad found a marijuana pipe in my room. He knew an ex-cop and made me go over to his house and talk to him. So I went over to his house and talked to him. It didn't really do anything; I just kinda blew it off. It wasn't anything.

I just kept drinking and smoking marijuana. The same old thing. In the eighth grade, I got caught again, but nothing happened. Parents just kinda shook their finger at me. Then, in the ninth grade, something big happened, but I can't remember.

I know I was selling marijuana at high school. Yeah, up in Tam. So my mom enrolled me into this outpatient rehab in San Rafael. I felt down all the time. It was all a game. In San Rafael, I stayed sober for a little while, but then I started to drink again.

I stopped smoking marijuana but I'd drink every day. Then I got suspended from the school and went to rehab again.

I stayed sober for a little while, then always returned to drinking and smoking marijuana. I started taking LSD with my friend. I just wouldn't go to school. I'd wake up in the morning, go straight to his house, and then take LSD all day. At rehab, after school, I told them I was sober, while I'd be like coming down off LSD. After a while, I didn't really like the acid, but I was always drinking. I got a dirty UA, a urine analysis. The test read positive for alcohol and cocaine. That was when I was going to rehab. It hit me pretty hard. For some reason, I felt caught. I was surprised.

People at school caught me breaking into cars, all sorts of stuff. Money, stereos, and stuff—I'd sell it at school. I had a regular for getting my coke. So, I was doing all that and then my mom said, you know, "They said you had a positive urine analysis for cocaine." I said, "Nope, not me. Test must be wrong or something."

My dad had stopped drinking, but wasn't going to AA. He just stopped. My mom has been sober for like a month longer than me. After I tested positive, the rehab guy said I needed something different, that I was just going into these groups and doing coke when I got out. He tried to talk to me, but I just said, "Shut the fuck up." I was so tense. He really didn't like me being there, so he said I better go off and stay away.

Then my mom drove me up to Washington state, and I stayed in this other place for twenty-eight days.

The first two weeks I was there, they wouldn't even let me smoke. I had to sneak tobacco in. It was a Twelve Step deal, and I only covered Steps One through Five. When I got out, I got the Steps from my sponsor, all twelve. So, my time there was a big part of my sobriety.

I was really angry there and broke a couple of doors. I was a punk kid.

I was selling cigarettes to kids outside at the Washington place, and eventually they caught me and for forty-eight hours they sent me to detox in Yakima. That hit me hard. "What the hell am I doing?" I thought.

I was a sixteen-year-old kid by myself in detox with a bunch of heroin addicts in a little town. It hit me hard. They picked me up after two days there. When I came back from that, I don't know what it was, but it just turned the rest of my stay around.

I wasn't angry, wasn't kicking doors down anymore, and wasn't punching walls. I guess I surrendered.

My mom was like two months sober when I got out. Mom

and Dad picked me up. They had been separated, and they told me on the way back that they figured that contributed to a lot of my anger.

I got out, went back home, and I just knew what to do. I know what I'm gonna do now that I've been to AA. That's where I belong. I belong in AA.

I started going on a regular basis and putting myself in front of people.

I got connected and started having fun. I was going to a meeting every day. I'd never done that before. I had fun, staying out late, drinking coffee and doing stuff. I was sitting out in front of this meeting place once and this guy came up to me and asked, "Do you have a sponsor?" I said, "Well, I just sat down last night, and this other guy came up with some people I'd like to be my sponsor." The guy said, "Well, go ask one." So I did.

I hooked up. I picked this sponsor because I think we related in the way we were drinking. I know it might make me seem like a racist, but people I had drunk with were all skinheads and stuff. I drank with older people.

I looked at this guy. I could just tell he had the same stuff as me in his past. He was like nine years sober and had tattoos all over his body. I thought he'd be a good sponsor for me.

I was full of fear, and he called me every day. So I worked through stuff with him. I never really believed in God or anything, or had any faith at all. I had this resentment against God, because if there's a God, why is all this bad stuff happening to me? Why is my life miserable?

I was working on the Second Step. I didn't get it. But I just did it. I don't know how. I just did it without even knowing. I'm grateful for that now. When I look back, I see this presence of a Higher Power in my life. I didn't even know. I didn't know it had happened. I kept working the Steps with my sponsor. I was going out for coffee almost every night of the week with a good bunch of guys. He asked me every day, "What are you doing responsibly?" It was great, just having coffee. It was a real spiritual thing.

I see guys about my age trying to pull me back in. I knew I couldn't see those guys anymore. It was really hard then, and my feelings were coming back real slow. With those guys I used to hang out with, I couldn't have made it.

So I just sat around the house. I raced my motorcycle, too. It was okay with my dad and my brother (my mom was always okay), but with all these feelings coming back it was terrible. I don't know how I did it. It was AA. All of a sudden I could talk, and I had real friends.

But drinking thoughts come up while everything's going well. I think, "Beer would really top this off." But I know I'd be right back where I was.

I know that now. You turn it over, like in the Steps, and things get better because it's not all on you. Like my anger. That was my fault and I'm sorry about that. I can turn it over. I want that to go away, along with the stuff about Dad. It will.

CHAPTER NINE

Suddenly I Could Talk

GROWING UP INCLUDED rooms full of light. Suddenly, we'd all be together, my mother and father and I, and the room would light up. It felt so good. There was an edge of sadness in it. That was later on, when I suspected that everything good would eventually go away.

But when I was really young, the feelings would suddenly flower. There was nothing like it. We'd play little games, maybe just throw a ball from chair to chair around the living room. It would usually be too late for me to be up. Maybe we'd just be back from the movies and nobody felt tired. Maybe we'd seen *Singin' in the Rain*. Maybe something good had happened that I knew nothing about, and there I'd be, bathing in this light, which was nothing but the three of us happy. I felt like I could just be the way I was and that would be fine. We'd laugh and love one another. It wasn't anything to do with communicating, or the deadly notion of "quality time." It was life, as it could be. It was silliness and laughter and grace. It was three human beings at their best. I tried all the time to re-create the moments as they got fewer and farther between.

Did Matt have times like these?

What if there hadn't been any? What about the kids who don't even have the memory of light? What about parents who didn't? What about the kids with parents who didn't and instead nurtured an avenging God? What about the utter sense of missed things and thwarted love?

Kids create explanations for what is missing. "These are my parents and they must love me. These are my parents and when I'm better they'll change. This is my life but I don't know the rules and nobody tells me. God is looking at me. What am I doing wrong?"

How many kids are in this landscape? Like the old comic book puzzles: How many faces can you find in this bush? What should we do? Build more jails?

I saw kids like Matt all the time when I worked in treatment. It was so hard for them to imagine that anybody cared that they were thrown back on the substance of themselves, a damaged substance. They'd come to believe in will, but didn't have any. They had pride, but it was as temporary as an overfilled balloon.

"Don't touch me because I need to be touched and I will not ask. I'm better than that. You don't know who I am, so fuck off."

The turning point happens in a house when everyone's working to stay alive by helping the one in the next chair to stay alive and God comes slipping in like a fine spring mist, an unusually breathable air.

It's such a delicate thing, watching a human being coming to the point of recognition, taking a breath of relief, smiling "hello" in a hallway.

If you want to feel God, go into a treatment program. Not a deluxe treatment center where the food is great and the landscaping, too, but one where the indigent come because the pain is too much, and even though they're almost dead, something is holding them up and not letting them die. False pride, maybe. Maybe a memory. Maybe a bit of light in the head that says, "No, stick around."

There's nothing wrong with the deluxe places, not if they work, but down at road level is where things are most palpable and the light coming up in the eyes has to be the light of God because nothing else is there but the empty place where the lost go.

A presence sometimes requires nothing at all but a modicum of care, one for the other. Three people trying to save themselves by saving each other are the three who are gathered in God's name. Then, he's always felt because he's always there, and always was.

I don't know where Matt went in his program and detox. I don't even know if he got it really, because he's so unused to speaking about his emotions. If you listen hard to a human soul trying to come into the world, there's something to be gained.

Looking through the transcript, trying to find the point of departure, there's just the voice, compelling in its odd, passive way. But do listen because there's a life, a person, and a soul here.

Something big happened, he said. What? This is his voice that won't disclose. Probably for him, there's never been any profit in telling anyone. It was like talking into the wind or sitting against the wall in the schoolyard while an extra cool wind blew.

I once heard an inarticulate guy say, "I wanted to save my ass but I found out it was attached to my soul."

Some can talk but find there's a gulf between their voices, talking, and the metallic weight and blankness of the pain. They can say how things happened, but somehow the words don't go anywhere or get out. It's what you hear in a bar, late, when the voices are loud but nothing is said. These are desperate efforts to explain in an empty place.

In the program where I worked, I remember a very nice kid in the program who was nineteen or twenty. He left the program and was dead by the following morning. In groups, he'd talk about his life with an absolute openness. He'd talk about a missing mother, a father who beat him up all the time, a discovery that alcohol was a door to a place where he was somebody and knew what to do.

He was heartbreaking because he'd started so young that he'd never had time to build himself a defense, a fake persona. When he was asked how he felt about his father he'd say, "Okay." He knew he must have been doing something wrong or his dad wouldn't have gotten so angry with him.

He thought that maybe his father had been trying to break him of something that wasn't right in him, something wrong, and strange. He thought it was his fault, and a certain blankness in his face said so. He left treatment because his girlfriend had called and said she was bored and was going out to get drunk. He'd gone to stop her because she was all he'd ever had. He'd spent his time planning an alternate life, an understandable life, and she'd smashed him between a tree and her car as she'd tried to drive past him to go get drunk.

He'd thought there was something wrong with him.

Matt doesn't have that kind of story, but there's something in his voice, as if the sheer weight of things not understood, or understood terribly, has made it hard for him to talk.

Matt doesn't talk, not really. He seems to be living in a foreign country when he's asked to talk about emotions and his sense of the world. His voice has one tone, never rising or falling. There are long silences where you wouldn't expect them, as if the sentences have no motive force and can just stop anywhere.

He, like most lost humans, thinks emotions can kill. All he'll say is "fucked-up" or "angry" to explain his feelings, as if these words were things that you walk into like a drifting cloud of gnats.

He's sometimes incoherent because he's swallowed a thought and doesn't know where to go. I had a counselor in treatment who would stop a faltering sentence in the middle and say, "What did you swallow? Come on, what did you just swallow? It won't kill you. Say it."

I very much want Matt to be okay, and I listen closely for the place where something may have happened. It's difficult to hear what happened because his voice is so even.

I hear Matt say, "Good bunch of guys. My sponsor asked me every day, 'What are you doing responsibly?' It was great, just having coffee. Real spiritual."

I hear the dignity of the child in that, and when I think about what Matt wants, there's a family in a kitchen late at night, and a little boy picked up and held tight in warm light, all of them loving each other, talking to each other.

I wish him all of that, which is what God is.

❧

Shari, who comes next, is tough in a way that Matt isn't. She's from a different time, when our vocabularies had yet to get sparse and jargon-ridden. She's from Massachusetts, but she could have been from Brooklyn. Women like her were all over when I was growing up. She was the Irish girl with the bright eyes to whom little attention was paid by anyone official but who labored along in a secret place, tough and forlorn. I think of my friend Carol, bright and sweet and shell-shocked, who wanted to go to college. Her father said, "What's the point? She'll just get married anyway." Her high school counselor came to see her parents, to plead, but no dice.

Carol did well, anyway, but the bars in Brooklyn were full of the women who didn't quite make it. That bar was every bar. I've remembered for thirty years a woman in a bar called Jack Storm's in San Francisco, way out by the ocean in the empty, wide avenues. I went in for a beer (that's always the euphemism), and there she was, dancing with the bartender. She was wearing a green satin dress and a gardenia on her shoulder. It must have been her birthday. There was one other guy in the place, way down at the end of the bar, and when the music ended she'd put in another quarter and he'd dance with her. The song was Dean Martin singing "Everybody Loves Somebody Sometime." I got out after I'd heard it three times. I can't remember any of them talking.

There was the woman in Moriarty's in Brooklyn, too, sharp and verbal and bright-eyed, sitting at the bar on Christmas Eve and playing "The Little Boy That Santa Claus Forgot," over and over again. She'd be up for mass in the morning, probably, walking down to the church with a thousand pounds of waste and misery in her, looking for something and finding the murmuring crowd and the same old sermon.

That was a different time, not much like Matt's. But the emptiness was the same; the vocabularies just hadn't shrunk to fit it yet.

After years, Shari found God singing in a choir, just like that. "Sure, I believe," she said.

What a relief.

CHAPTER TEN

Shari

I WAS A HONEYMOON BABY. I was born in 1948, nine months and one day after my parents' first night together at a hotel in New York City.

We lived in a blue-collar town in Massachusetts; my father was a retail salesman. He was Irish English, and my mother was French Canadian. Her God was to be feared, and she let me know that.

I grew up going to church on a regular basis, dressed in my finest. We lived in a six-family duplex in a poor area, and when I was five we moved into a low-income housing project. My father had been in the armed services and was automatically entitled to an apartment.

I had two sisters, Susan and Kathy. When I was a little girl, if I fell or anything happened to me, I'd run to my mother to say, "Mommy, Mommy, I hurt my knee." She'd always say, "Well, God is punishing you. You must have done something wrong."

I grew up with this fear of God, even though I never really believed. I went to Saint Anne's Academy, from kindergarten through high school. I grew up with nuns who shamed me.

They beat me on the knuckles with a ruler, and in the third grade my teacher pulled my hair and went, "Ew, your hair is oily." I'd had a cold that week and didn't wash my hair on purpose, because my mother had told me not to.

I was precocious, and I always felt shamed. I wanted to speak, communicate, and socialize, but I was always put down for it. I got good grades except for Cs and Ds in conduct. My effort was always A plus and the lowest mark I ever got was a B minus.

I was afraid of school. I was anxious all the time. My sisters and I were project kids and were never accepted, especially when we didn't have the clothes the others had.

My mother loved to entertain the priests at home. They'd drink port in little red glasses that looked . . . not like chalices, but like something holy. I found the whole thing sacred somehow. Their personalities changed when they drank the wine.

I was very shy, and when they came over, I'd hide behind the sofa. I was afraid of the priests for some reason. I wouldn't have a good reason till later.

I always went to communion. I was always in a state of grace, because I went to confession before communion and did my penance on Saturday afternoons. The older I got, the less comfortable I was, because I could feel myself trying to believe in God. Everyone around me seemed to believe. I faked it so I wouldn't be alone.

I began to feel like a fraud as my hormones started to rage. I remember sitting in religion class and not believing and wanting to tell everybody off. I wanted to shout that it was all nonsense, that I didn't believe in the Holy Trinity.

I thought maybe, maybe, there was a Creator. I got that part, but I didn't get the Son of God bit. I believed he was just a good man. I absolutely didn't get the Trinity.

I'd gone to my first communion when I was six, and by the time I was twelve, I was confessing the same thing over and over again. Inside, I knew that I was going to commit the same sin that night. I felt very, very uncomfortable.

The way the nuns and the headmaster treated all of us was awful. We'd be called out of class for something we'd done outside of class, even in our neighborhoods. The headmaster would come in, and someone would have to stand up and be humiliated. I knew about humiliation, and it enraged me. I had serious rages, and the idea that this son of a bitch could claim to be a man of God and spend his time humiliating children just flamed in my head.

Once a quieter boy in class, God love him, got up and said, "I've had it. I can't take it anymore," and he walked out.

The whole class burst into cheers.

We were prisoners. My first-grade teacher was my fourth-grade teacher, my sixth-grade teacher, my English teacher, and my French teacher. This woman did not like me. No matter what I did, no matter what I said.

When I was thirteen, I decided I didn't want to go to Saint Anne's. I wanted to go to South High with my friends. By this time, we were living in a second project that was even farther away from the school than the first. I'd make breakfast and lunch sometimes because my mother was depressed and couldn't do it. She was hung over, I know that now, but then her depression was a great mystery. No one thought it odd that I was taking care of my sisters from the time I was five. Parents sick in the morning weren't unusual in my world.

At thirteen, I went to work at the rectory at Notre Dame Cathedral. The pastor there had been at our house a lot, drinking port with my mother. I had no particular trepidation about going to the rectory with him. I remember watching Lee Harvey Oswald get shot on TV in the rectory after mass.

About the third time I was there, he tried to fondle my breasts. He did fondle me once, because he caught me by surprise. I wasn't sure what he was going to do. I ran around the dining-room table, running and running and running till I'd exhausted him. Then I ran out the door, and I told my mother I'd never go back. I said, "I just don't like it there."

There was another priest, too, who was an instructor at an expensive Catholic boys' school. He introduced me to young men who had money. That was something I wanted. I knew one thing for sure, I didn't want to be poor anymore. I didn't want my parents' life anymore. I didn't want to fight about money and break things in the kitchen.

That priest tutored me in Latin for three years, and everything was fine. Then when I turned sixteen, he started holding and kissing me, telling me how lonely he was. I didn't run away, but I felt guilty and ashamed. I'd pretend to be sick when he called.

However, like I said, he did introduce me to a lot of the Assumption boys. I'd meet them downtown and go to the movies. They'd have to take me home on the bus. When they'd see the projects where I lived, they'd never call back. Not ever, not one of them. After about six months of that, I was deeply ashamed of everything about me.

Everything was starting to revolve around material things. I was really set on having things and never having to feel poor again.

I stopped going to church unless they made me. I never went to communion. The nuns would ask why, and I'd say, "I'm not in a state of grace."

The entrance exam for Saint Anne's High School took about three hours. Since I didn't want to go anyway, I just sat there during the exam and did nothing until the last half hour. Then I opened the book and filled it in: A, B, C, D; A, B, C, D.

I failed, and I was thrilled, because it meant I could go to public school. I was psyched. This was January. In May, just before I got out of junior high, I was called to the headmaster's office. My parents were there, and I knew right away I was dead meat. I could feel it.

Everyone knew my mother. She was very popular and never showed a character defect in public. She saved them up for us.

She abused us, mostly me, physically. I still have scars on my head. She beat me with a strap and so did my father, especially when he was drunk.

If I came home with all As, my father would say, "Why aren't they A pluses?" The terrible thing is, I don't think my house was much different from anyone else's. I did then, and it made me cringe, but I found out later, along the way, that most of my friends had the same stuff going on.

My father would never compliment me. I don't remember him ever saying he loved me. I don't even remember him ever saying that he liked me or that I looked nice or that I was smart. Nothing. I never got a compliment from him. My mother wasn't much better. She would never say she was sorry. Between the two of them, I didn't get much affection.

My mother would give me a little affection when I was the house angel and took care of the things she couldn't, but when I did something wrong, she'd take it back again and punish me like six or eight weeks at a time. Most of my friends would be grounded for only one or two days. She liked to ground me because it was a great way to keep me home so she wouldn't have to do the housework.

Anyway, when I saw my parents at the headmaster's office, I knew I was gone. He said, "Shari, I'd like you to sit down." Then he said, "I've talked to your parents and we're willing to give you a trial here at Saint Anne's Academy High School. But we're going to put you in the general class."

So I ended up in the general class for about two weeks, and then went into the commercial class for about four weeks. After that, I went into the college prep class. I was not happy. I was abusive to the teachers in religion. I'd sit in the back of the class and read existentialism. There was a book on Sartre, and I'd make sure the nuns were watching while I'd read it over and over again. I believed I existed and that was it. I didn't believe in anything. I believed that my spirit would die when I died, and that was the bottom line.

I really had no God in my life except for the big papier-mâché guy pushed at the church. I wasn't even trying anymore. Everything was easier once I'd made a decision not to believe in God. It seemed that way. I felt less guilty.

At about the same time, my drinking increased. I had experimented a little bit before, but I really became a weekend drinker when I was fifteen. I would go over to my girlfriend's house, and by the time I was sixteen or seventeen, I was pretty deeply involved with young men who were twenty-four, twenty-five. They were the fast crowd, the Corvette Club.

I'd tell my mother I was going over to my best friend's house for the weekend and that we were going to church on Sunday, but instead I'd be down on Rhode Island drag racing with the Corvette Club. My nickname was Jailbait, because I was underage.

I had three boyfriends in the club. I was always there because they bought me alcohol. I'd get sick a lot, but they didn't care. They'd clean me and fix me up. I was a trophy.

I was spiritually dead. While I was out on errands for my

homeroom class, the nun would have the kids pray for my soul. A senior told me, "Every time you leave, we pray for your soul. We're not supposed to tell you." I was really angry. I confronted the nun and said, "How dare you do that? It's none of your business what I believe and don't believe."

In my junior year, the faculty had to vote on whether or not I'd be part of the National Honor Society. I lost. A nun told me that the headmaster was the one who blocked me.

At seventeen, I had a boyfriend who'd pick me up and share a six-pack with me in the morning. So by the time I got to school, I already had three beers in my stomach.

Religion was my first class, and I didn't like the priest who taught it. Our class was on marriage when I was a senior, and I argued with him all the time. He said that a woman, a wife, should always be ready to forgive her husband enough to perform her sexual chores with him.

I was outraged at this. I believed that that was not a woman's place and that I was not put on this planet to feed a man's ego by forgiving if I wasn't ready to forgive. We'd go round and round and round. Everything he said, I'd have an answer for.

I was inducted into the National Honor Society in my senior year, which was helpful because it got me scholarships. All through high school, I'd worked at a downtown low-income retail store. I got to be an assistant personnel manager and assistant merchandise manager. I could be really responsible, if you paid me.

At the end of June 1966, my parents were looking at a bungalow that was right on the way to the state college I'd picked. I thought it was a great place, but my mother said, "Well, how are we going to afford it? I don't have any money for a down payment."

So I wrote out a check for $1,600 and said, "I'll do it." I gave them my scholarship money. She paid me back in a year and a half. These people could never save two nickels, so I was suddenly very powerful in the family. I was always bringing things home, from the time I started working—clothes for the family, desks, chairs, pictures. I became the mother figure, and I was strict like the nuns because that's all I knew.

My sisters were very resentful of me because I had so much power in the family. I'm still working on that issue with them. With my mother too, who still resents my getting power, even though she abdicated hers.

I went to college and got raped at the end of my freshman year by a blind date. I said, "The hell with it," and went about my business. I had a 3.78 average that year. I wasn't going to let a jerk derail me.

As a sophomore, my drinking became really bad, and I almost flunked out. I could drink any guy in my freshman and sophomore class under the table except for one. My nickname was Pegleg, and I liked it.

By the time I was nineteen, I'd been introduced to marijuana and black tar opium, though my drug of choice was always alcohol. It was more accessible, it tasted better, and I had a personality that needed to be calmed and sedated.

I married a man whom I'd known for three weeks. He was from Shaker Heights, Ohio. I went to his sister's wedding on a whim, and he asked me to marry him three weeks later.

"Good!" my father said to him. "I'm glad you're taking her out of the house."

My middle sister, Susan, waited till I got married, then screamed at me, "How could you leave me! You and I were supposed to get an apartment together. I'm almost out of high school. How could you do this?"

I took her into the bathroom at the reception and said, "I love you, but I'm married now. I wish you'd said something."

My mother's choice as to who would preside at the wedding was the pastor who'd chased me around the table. The priest from the boys' school was my choice. They were the only two priests I knew. So, which of the perpetrators do I pick? I told my mother that the pastor would not be presiding at my wedding, and she asked, "Why not?" I said, "Because he chased me around the rectory and tried to fondle and kiss me."

"I don't believe you," she said. "I just don't believe that he would do something like that."

Why would I make up a story like that, especially around something as important as my wedding? "Well, I want the other priest, Alfred," I said. So he performed the ceremony. I was uncomfortable.

Mark, my new husband, was an atheist and a socialist. I thought I'd be getting into a wealthy family but found out he didn't want to live like his parents. I'd never known anyone like him because I'd never been out of town except for a bus trip to New York with my aunt.

We discussed labor history in our home, and we had meetings. We all read *Labor's Untold Story* and then *Das Kapital*. Mark was a Lenin fan and wanted nothing to do with Chinese or Cuban communism. I was more of a socialist. I figured half a person's taxes should go to the well-being of all.

I still believe that. I believed in the graduated income tax and universal health care and things like that. Those ideas fed me in lieu of any kind of spirituality. I was doing something for myself and the community, and I felt a part of the community.

I liked being with Mark because he opened up worlds for me that I'd never come in contact with before. We went on train rides. His parents had a place in Delray Beach, Florida.

He did reject a lot of that, the money, but the material stuff was always there, gnawing at me. I really wanted it. Like I said, I didn't ever want to feel deprived again.

When I became a teacher, I taught at a school open from seven o'clock in the morning till ten o'clock at night. It offered health care, counseling, and federal government services. We also had a reading program for kids.

I became the co-chair of the model cities program and started seeing the director, a married man. We designed a trip to go out to three different schools in Michigan. We drank the whole way there, the whole time we were there, and the whole way back. I was functional then, drinking or dry. I could work, and I had an incredible amount of stamina. I was up and coming. I wanted notoriety.

I became a rep the first day I was teaching. We had a strike vote—whether we were going to accept a contract or reject it. I got voted the rep.

"Let's vote for Shari. She's got a mouth and she'll use it," the sixth-grade rep said.

So that's how I was elected. I changed the bylaws from being sexist to using "he/she," and when they complained that it was cumbersome I said, "Well, the majority of the teachers in the district are women, so why don't we just use 'she'?" So they decided that "he/she" was fine. I became the first female union president at twenty-five years old. I was the youngest by twelve years. I felt comfortable and powerful, so who needed God? I was a god. I was a goddess. I could get things done.

We sued the district over pregnancy leave and won. I thought, "I did it, it was me." I was in the newspaper a lot and on local TV.

When the affirmative action issue came up I had a problem.

I was evasive and ambiguous because I had to go against my own philosophical beliefs. My substitute for spirituality was my sense of community and my conscience. I felt guilty when I went against it. Although I didn't believe in God, I had a truly strong value system.

I went to therapy from the time I was twenty-four because I knew underneath something was wrong with me. My therapist said, "Well, you never talk to me about anything except drinking. You have an emotional life, a physical life, but you don't have a spiritual life."

"So what?" I said.

"Well, most people do talk about God and most people have some sort of religion," he replied. "Do you ever meditate?"

I said, "No, I can't. My mind races too much. I can't meditate."

Once I was sitting in his waiting room and saw the Serenity Prayer on his wall. The Serenity Prayer says, "God grant me the serenity to accept the things I cannot change, the courage to change the things I can, and the wisdom to know the difference." Now, after five years of visiting him, I had never noticed the prayer on the wall. And at thirty-one, I had never heard of the prayer. "That's an interesting prayer that you have on that wall," I said. "I don't have the wisdom to know the difference."

I never could delegate responsibility. It had to be me. I had to be the one in control, in charge all the time, because I had no trust. I grew up not trusting people. I had no reason to trust.

I drank all the time. I was smoking three packs of Marlboros a day and drinking a half gallon of wine mixed with liberal amounts of cocaine. In some odd way, it felt like I was trying to drink myself sober.

From when I started in AA until I was a year sober, I cried

through every single meeting. I saw the word *God* on the wall, in the Steps, and I said, "If I have to do this, I'm not going to be able." Then I said, "What's my alternative?"

I got a male sponsor because when I got a woman sponsor, we were codependents. He was an older man, and I was married again by that time, so he asked my husband for permission to sponsor me, which was totally interesting. That's the way they did it back then.

I wanted to stick with the women. I felt I was supposed to. Yet I had no respect for the women because I was stronger than they were. They were whiny, I thought, and I didn't like whiny women.

I believed the power in the Second Step was the program— the outreach and the sponsor and the socializing. When I got to the Third Step, turning my life over to the care of God as I understood him, well, I didn't like the "him" to begin with. I couldn't get past that. So, I just skipped the Step.

My sponsor would tell me to get on my knees and ask God to remove my compulsion to drink, to keep me sober and straight one day at a time. I would tell my sponsees the same thing, but I didn't do it. I acted like I did it.

I got involved in service work right away. I was used to the governance and power stuff. When I tried to change things, I got booted out. Nicely and gently, but booted out.

After three months of sobriety, I decided that I was going to write my Fourth Step. My sponsor said, "I don't think you're ready." I said, "Well, I think I'm ready." I bought myself some lined paper, opened up the booklet, and wrote the first two paragraphs. Then, I froze and couldn't go any further. I was three and a half years sober before I could do another Fourth Step.

George, my third sponsor, said to me, "When are you going to do your Fifth Step?"

"I don't know," I said. He didn't know I hadn't done my Fourth. He wanted me to do it with someone else, because he wasn't comfortable listening to a woman's Fifth Step.

There were priests in the program, and I picked one of them. We were all very Catholic. At the time, 55 percent of the town was Catholic. I made a date for it. So I went through the whole thing, and I managed.

I didn't feel any kind of spiritual stuff afterward. I reflected, just like the Big Book says, and felt I'd built a solid foundation, but without the God piece.

Everybody in the program was my Higher Power, but God was not my Higher Power. I was envious of the people who did get the God stuff. I wanted what they had.

I was living with Lenny, my second husband. I did a lot of people pleasing. Lenny and I taught catechism for two or three years to freshman and sophomore high school girls.

I knew something wasn't working, though, and when there were marriage problems I went to the priest, who said, "I can't help you."

I was angry. I thought, "I've given this time, and I'm trying, and I'm going to church, and I'm trying to get it. Then the priest says he can't help me. What?" I got divorced and went to Al-Anon and Overeaters Anonymous. I moved to Pittsfield, and that was the first time I was ever alone. Nobody knew me. I wasn't in the papers, and I didn't chair the Democratic District Three Committee.

I was just alone. I was a nobody.

"If I'm lonely," I thought, "maybe I'll get it."

And I did, a little bit. I got a concept of a Higher Power for a short bit of time. When you're alone, a Higher Power doesn't seem strange at all.

Then my ex didn't want me to see the grandchildren. It was Christmas. I needed to see them. Maybe I didn't want to drink, but I did want to suck on a Valium. I needed help, but I didn't turn to God. I turned instead to a psychiatrist.

We talked about codependency and how it was going to be worse when I got to California, where I had just taken a job. He said, "They're just different in California. There are loyalties in Massachusetts that you won't find. You're going to find more betrayal there." He was right.

I moved to L.A. The buildings were huge and I felt small. I was intimidated by my job. I felt small in every way. In time, doors were opened for me, and I felt the power again. The job was my Higher Power. I went to meetings, was ten years sober, yet I'd never had a Higher Power.

So? So what?

You know how that sounds in your own ears?

I hadn't had a compulsion in ten years except for the Valium. I believed I could survive as long as I wanted to.

I got sick and was diagnosed in 1995 with fibromyalgia and chronic exhaustion. And TMJD (temporomandibular joint disorder), which means I grind my teeth. I've been doing that since I was a kid, but now it was really, really bad. I couldn't sleep. My life was totally nuts. I would cry about my job at meetings. People were sick of it. There was a period of wanting to die.

Finally, on a Sunday afternoon, I called up my insurance company. I told the woman who answered about my illness, wanting to die, and AA. What I got back was, "Why don't you see a psychiatrist?"

So I did. I didn't pack anything. I wanted them to lock me up. I had fantasized suicidal thoughts before, but this time there were no fantasies. I was extremely depressed. Nothing seemed to be completed in my job. It just went on and on and on.

I wanted to rest. They locked me up for seventy-two hours. When I got out, I took a two-month leave of absence from my job. Diagnosed with bipolar disorder, I was put on lithium. I had anxiety disorder, too. With the medication, things seemed to be going smoothly, though something was still missing.

In September and October of 2000, I had another breakdown. I was manic. The lithium had stopped working. I fell in a pothole. My car was stolen.

I was now "desperate as the dying." I needed something outside of myself and it wasn't my AA sponsor, the other women in the program, meetings, or my own will.

I had gone to Glide Memorial Church a few times with a friend. I remembered the sense of love I'd felt there, and how impressed I'd been by their programs for the poor and at-risk.

Most of all I remembered the Glide choir—the Ensemble, they were called—and how they looked and sounded, rocking the house every Sunday with gospel. So out of nowhere, I went to the 9:00 and 11:00 A.M. services.

It was very odd. I felt at home in church. The church school had been the place of my most intense humiliations. In the past, at church I felt embarrassment for my poverty, my inability to fit in, and my loss of innocence. But this was a different church, and the choir lifted itself up and flew. I asked how I could be in the choir (which was a much deeper question for me than they probably knew). They told me to audition on Wednesday, and I became an alto in the choir. Finally, I could open my throat wide and let the stuff out.

I thought, "This is the ticket." And it was. I had a home where I was free, and I felt joy in praising God for the first time since I was a child. Singing God's praises was like praying.

I thought about what it meant to turn my will and life over to a Higher Power—twenty years late. I was building a personal relationship with the God of my own understanding. I was slowly relying more now on a Higher Power for answers to my life.

I was feeling safer in the world. In the choir, other human beings put their feelings out to God in a joyful, ecstatic way. Everything seemed to go out of me, and it was all perfectly good. It was high, elevated music. Other people were joined to me and the voices of everything lovely in humankind. I wasn't alone.

I didn't have to pretend to be tough. That's how I'd got by before, saying, "Watch out, I'm tough." I had stood in opposition and gathered up power.

Singing was something else again, and I felt myself drawn back into the human, which is a different strength altogether.

I had started going to women's meetings, too. I finally got a good sponsor who didn't believe any of my bullshit and who let me know that I was not her favored, special one.

Women's meetings, no distractions, no men, and singing in the choir to God—this was the kind of spirituality I could stick with. I began to feel that something else was ruling the world.

I'd lost all my jobs and the sense of power that went with them. On paper, my situation was still desperate as the dying, but there was something else. For me, losing everything was a good thing.

After a while, I didn't have the stamina to go to Glide anymore because of the fibromyalgia. It was exhausting. I got tired, too, of all the rah-rah praise for the heads of the church.

I remembered my catechism: "Thou shalt have no other Gods before me."

Finally, finally, finally I felt totally powerless—over myself, over people, places, and things. There now existed a power greater than myself. I became less selfish and less self-reliant. I became more giving.

Unconditional love—because of it, I felt a freedom that I'd never felt before, and I still feel it. It's such a wonderful gift. I was twenty and a half years sober before I found a Higher Power. I thought I'd never get it. I'd given up.

It wasn't until the material things, the things that had been so important to me, were yanked away that I was able to finally meditate, listen, and refuse the door with the locks and chains. Today, I walk through the open doors. If they're closed or just ajar, they're not meant for me.

I gave the Salvation Army my beautiful furniture. It had cost me twenty-five thousand dollars, but I gave it away because I didn't want it anymore. I didn't want the money.

Instead, what I wanted was someone without money to have my furniture and use it. I replaced it all with stuff from IKEA. I'm thrilled. Nothing I have is overwhelming anymore. I got my day bed for twenty-nine dollars.

Sometimes I put on a tape from Glide for the spirituality. I find myself touched by a deep God, a visceral God. In my gut, I feel a power greater than me. Sometimes I call her "Goddess." I feel like the place where I live is in concert with my spirit. My God! I feel like I'm living as a spiritual person. I don't feel burdened.

My dog had been in the shelter, had been abused, and I was able to rescue it and give it structure and love. I'm able to have a dog and not abuse it. In my family abuse trickles through everything like blood.

My mother still abuses my stepfather. She kicked him in the ribs on their fifteenth wedding anniversary and broke three of them. My middle sister has one child. She named her after me and has abused her physically and emotionally. My youngest sister got clean and sober but then turned her back on AA. I know she abuses her husband. She has a son, too.

Me? I don't have a name for God, I just know and trust.

Something in my head told me that sobriety was a gift to begin with, but I couldn't get my head and my heart together. I couldn't feel it physically.

I'm consistent now. I'm not up and down anymore. I'm me. I have personality defects, and I'll probably have them for the rest of my life. But I don't have the anger and the rage that kept me away from God. I'm getting better all the time.

CHAPTER ELEVEN

Finally, Finally, Finally

TEN YEARS AGO, I wrote in a poem, "The deepest sensuality comes with the coming of grace to the unyielding." It was a complete statement of the truth, as I knew it, and nothing in these interviews would alter it.

When I surrendered to God, I had a sudden access to reality. Things I'd pushed around in my mind to keep them out of the foreground became nothing at all in terms of either weight or fearfulness. When I keep trying to offer my life without recourse to ambiguity or decoration, everything that's ever happened to me becomes bearable, watchable, unembarrassing—a nourishing substance I can pass on as you might a simple warning: Here be monsters.

There's an implicit balance, and while shame or humiliation may still flare up out of nowhere when I least expect it, it's bearable. I can see myself for the fool I am and be astonished at the shallowness that lets remembered embarrassments hurt even more than the pain I've caused others while running on personality and obfuscation.

It's possible to get used to trying to tell the truth, and it feels good. Successful or unsuccessful, the effort by itself is calming and balancing. I once heard a drunk say that when drunk, he was either too big or too small in the street. That's the shifting world of the personality and the false ego.

Shari's story contains the lies we pass on to our kids. The lies are told for our convenience or to hide our weaknesses. What kind of twisting does a human endure before he tells his kid that God is fear and punishment?

How could a God who knows everything be feared? Could there be any weakness beyond his complete understanding?

I have a personal horror of the depredations of organized religion, which I largely see as a structure designed and built by those who've discovered that power attaches to careers in hierarchical interpretation. This judgment may be unfair of me, because in religious congregations are people of enormous goodwill and faith, and I'm sure that when a man or woman comes to God, the church of one's childhood is perhaps the one natural, accessible place to go.

Nevertheless, any human structure that teaches the fear of God perpetuates distance from God. This is utterly artificial. Pity us all. Shari's first immersion in God was fear: "I don't have to beat you up. God will do it for me."

In the Gospels are two instances of Christ's anger: one against the money changers in the temple and the other against anyone who would damage a child.

The second isn't even anger, which is after all passionate, but a simple, cold, and unyielding statement: "It were better a millstone . . . "

Are the trappings of power, authority, willfulness, and humiliation in the Gospels?

It's hard to say much of anything about sex as a dirty chore, rage as sustenance, judgment as satisfaction, or forgiveness as acquiescence. Everything beautiful and real in life seems written down with a line drawn through it.

Think about Shari's family without the crutches and the filigree and the need to inflict. What if her mother had remembered her own misery one morning and decided to stop passing it on? What if she'd said, "God, I'm so sorry. Honey, I'm so sorry. I love you so much, but I never know what to do." I know what happens when I hear this. Everything opens and the knot at the base of the throat turns to tears.

All the material is right at hand. None of us wants misery extended. None of us wants to spend a life in fearful hiding. None of us wants our kids to be as miserable as we were. We hear that all the time in meetings: "Most of all, I wanted to make sure that my kids wouldn't go through what I went through. I didn't want to do to them what my parents did to me."

When you work in treatment, you discover that drunks are intensely moral people and judge themselves by a high standard. Of course, this can produce self-loathing and the desperate mental strain of trying to sustain two overwhelmingly contradictory beings in one body. It isn't unusual for lapsed Catholics like Shari to want to have a priest hear her Fifth Step. There's the tradition of secrecy and the memory of successful lying. Or it is forgiveness.

The process that leads away from the demented begins with rejoining humanity. Singing in a choir, maybe. Sitting in a roomful of people who are all trying to tell the truth.

You start to see the others, hear them when they say how they see you, and understand that there were things you tried to hide from them. We hide an even greater volume of things from ourselves.

It's odd. It isn't necessary to like the members of a group, but when humans gather together to help each other, without judging, love is there. This is not a process restricted to drunks. This is how sight becomes vision, how God enters our bodies. Then someone gets one foot out of the machinery and says, "Look, things don't have to be this way."

Harry M. told me not to worry about the bad meetings, that the percentage of assholes in AA was exactly the same as the percentage of assholes in the general population. It wasn't good, he said, not to grant an asshole and ourselves the possibility of change.

Personality isn't much. It jumps up and down, twists its face and howls, but when you get through all the noise, it's a construct of odd-angled nailings and pastings lurching along on rickety wheels.

And when it shifts or slips, as it can in a room full of people trying to tell the truth, there's a space for a moment where there is no fear. You think, "Oh, sure, there I am," and God fills the space. God grants the grace to see ourselves as others see us, and understand our likenesses in a plain light. Shari won or was granted that understanding.

Some things will always hurt because that's the nature of the world. When the hurt changes, as it can and did for Shari, a voice comes with the change that lets the newfound peace or understanding be passed along. It's very beautiful.

❧

Here begins Angela's story. She rents a house in Bel Marin Keys. It was built by a developer who carved out canals and cul-de-sacs around the house. The motif is tropical, and we sit out back in a lanai of sorts, surrounded by plants. There are boats moored across the water in the backyard. Angela has brown hair and eyes. She looks a bit like the young Debbie Reynolds.

CHAPTER TWELVE

Angela

I'M A TWENTY-THREE-YEAR-OLD white female who grew up in California. My mother raised my sister and me as a single parent. She had me at eighteen and my sister at nineteen. As little girls, we were moved around a lot because our father was a violent alcoholic. We had to move. We grew up really poor.

My grandparents, unhappy that my mom had us at such a young age, disowned my mother after my sister and I were born.

On my father's side, they're this huge Irish Catholic family. They weren't happy either. So it was just my mother, my sister, and me—the three of us. We tried to give each other love and be strong.

My father left when I was eighteen months old, right after my sister had been born. He was a man who would get drunk, break into the house, rape my mother, and then hide in the closet. He'd stalk her inside the house. That's why we moved around a lot. He did really psycho stuff. I remember not being able to have friends come over at night because we'd fear that if my father found out where we were living, he'd start breaking in again.

There wasn't any God or Higher Power, besides my dad, in our house. We didn't practice any religion. Mother taught us that religion was bad because my father and his family were Catholic and none of them were there for us after we were born.

We never went to church. When I got to be about twelve, I became curious and wanted to know what church was like. So once I went to church by myself on Christmas Eve to see what it was like. I don't know what I thought. It was strange.

Growing up, I was angry and sad because I didn't have my father. My mother drank a lot, too, and partied. She was more like a friend than a mother to me and my sister. I hate when I hear people say, "Oh, my mother and I are friends."

We didn't have much guidance. We got to do whatever we wanted. I grew up really fast, looking for attention and love from men. I was looking for something or someone to take me out of myself.

I started flirting with the older guys who lived in our apartment building. I experimented at an early age with sex. It wasn't that I had sex, but that I'd flirt and put myself out there. At twelve, my sister and I began to drink alcohol and smoke marijuana. When my mother found out, she said she'd prefer if we did it with her instead of outside the house.

By the time I was thirteen, I thought I was pretty great. I was an A student. I played basketball and was a cheerleader and had a lot going for me. I was successful in sports and school, had good positive friends in my life, and good relationships with my teachers and mentors. But I was using drugs. Like I said, it was at home with Mom.

I was pretty great on the outside. Inside, I was angry that my father wasn't there and that my mother had different boyfriends at the house all the time. I think now I was mostly sad, but I acted it out as anger. My sister and I would just fight with other kids in the neighborhood. We'd steal from stores.

I was thirteen years old.

Before long, I was smoking marijuana every day. I didn't

care about school anymore. I had my first relationship with an older man. He was seventeen.

The relationship was abusive. For the next two and a half years he beat and raped me. I got damaged. I stayed in the relationship because I got lost in it. He cheated on me all the time, but I stayed with him, thinking I could change him, thinking that he'd fix me somehow and make everything wonderful. I needed to be fixed, and I thought a man could do it. I started using speed and cocaine and stopped going to high school. I slept around with other men. I'm really, *really* lucky that I'm not HIV positive because I didn't use protection at all.

I slept around and afterward felt horrible. I continued to use, and by the time I was fifteen, I had dropped out of high school and was on probation.

I ran away because I didn't want to deal with the pain inside. I didn't want to deal with my boyfriend anymore, either. He didn't care for me, love me, or fix me. I met this older man who was thirty-six and thought maybe he could fix everything. He was married, had three kids, but I didn't know that.

He'd just left his wife. I was fifteen and had moved to the city with him, where I began smoking crack. He gave me the freedom, I thought. He let me run away from my problems. When I found out he was married, I left him and ended up living in the Mission District in a crack house where we bought our stuff.

I was a little girl living in San Francisco all by myself. The people who came in and out of the house were violent, felons and criminals. I was so grateful and amazed that I didn't get hurt by any of them. It came to my mind that something loved me.

It was a wonder that I wasn't raped. The things I saw.

I was hitting bottom for the first time, but there was

something there I couldn't quite make out. It didn't make any sense, because I couldn't attach it to anything. I had this sense way down inside that something loved me. I was so alone, and I was such a little girl with all these older men. There had to be something or someone, I thought.

After I got clean, I realized fully that something had taken care of me.

My mother was looking for me. The police were looking for me. My mother hired someone to look for me, while I was hiding in this dark, dark crack house.

People would come in and out twenty-four hours a day. I didn't sleep. One night I brought a photograph of my sister and me as little girls to the bathtub. I just sat in the water looking at it. I broke down and cried because I realized that I wanted my innocence back. I wanted my life back. You know what I mean?

It was an awakening for me. I had that picture of the two of us as young girls, and I *wanted that*. We looked so pure, but there I was in this evil bathtub. I realized that my life was a mess. I couldn't run away now from that realization and the pain of who I was.

I was lost, completely lost. I couldn't get out of the tub. I was just crying—we looked so *nice* in the picture, but something had happened. I called a friend of my mother's, and he came and picked me up. So there were people willing to help when I was almost gone. They loved me and helped me when I didn't love myself. That was a miracle. I saw God in other people, and that's how I became spiritual. I found God in other people.

My sister and I alone in a picture. We'd been so hopeful, so nice.

By this time, I was anemic, and very, very thin because I never ate. So I slept for a couple of days. I ate and ended up calling my mother because that was the agreement we made—that I'd call my mother.

I turned myself in to juvenile hall because I was on probation and there was a warrant out. By this time I was so defeated. I just wanted help.

In 1995, I stayed in juvenile hall for a couple months. They wanted to send me to rehab in the Bay Area, but I knew if I was sent anywhere around where I grew up I'd run away and use again. I wanted to go far away. They sent me to Colorado for a year and a half. It was a lockdown facility for girls.

I needed it. I worked on myself a lot. Not completely, but it gave me the time to not use, to be myself, and to try to get to know who I was.

I graduated a year and a half later. It wasn't the Twelve Steps or recovery but a girls' lockdown. I was still so afraid of doing something wrong.

It wasn't just the drug problem. There were things much deeper. When I graduated I was still afraid, so I asked my probation officer if I could go to a drug recovery center. I was so scared to be outside.

I ended up going to the Thunder Road adolescence treatment program for about six months, and that's where I really began getting to know who I was, getting more spiritual, getting to know God.

To this day, I don't have a name for God. I just know that there's something out there that's all loving. Sometimes I see it in the ocean; sometimes I see it in other people.

At Thunder Road, there were people I used to call angels. They were other recovering alcoholics and addicts who had been sober for twenty years. And they dedicated their lives to helping us.

I had a counselor named Ernie M. who taught me to love myself. He couldn't really make me love myself, but he made me go to women's meetings and made me do so much writing and work on myself.

He gave me the strength to keep moving. That's when I began to start to really believe in God. I had never got love like his. I had never had someone who really cared about me that way. I couldn't care for myself that way.

Without any other motives or intentions or wanting anything from me, he just wanted to be there, to help, to get to know who I was. I began to grow. That was really painful, because the memories were so close. They all said, "You're worthless."

I remember when I took my first AIDS test, *knowing* that I was going to be HIV positive. But I wasn't.

I've had a lot of friends die or go to prison. I asked myself, "How could I have made it if there wasn't *something?*" I was a little girl sitting nearly dead in a bathtub in a crack house. No one's life is worth anything in a crack house. There was *something.*

There was no way in hell that I could have made it out of there on my own. I was this anemic, crazy little kid in a jungle with people who hurt others for nothing, just because they felt like it. I didn't get raped and never worked on the street. There were plenty who did get raped, and worse. Girls died. I couldn't understand why it hadn't been me.

All I knew was that God loved them, too.

At one moment, there was nothing, and then there was something. All I had to do was let it in. I'd looked at myself and my sister and remembered how we'd been and how I'd wanted to be. Deep in the heart was the girl who I still was. Does that make sense?

Back from Thunder Road, I had one more year of high school left. I was afraid. I didn't want to go back to my original high school and be around those people anymore. It's not that they were any worse than me. They just hadn't found the way out. I just couldn't *be* there. It was too dangerous, and the memories were too evil. I decided to go to a sobriety high school. That's where I met my friend Clara. To this day, she has loved me and given me strength when I was weak. I see God in her. I do.

People can be so beautiful, and I aspire to be like them.

When I came home, my mother was still using drugs. My father was homeless and dying of cirrhosis of the liver. I know that they have to go their own ways, and I pray for them.

There are still times when I feel so alone. Suddenly, there's nobody, and it's just like it was when I was little. That passes, and I know it will pass.

I went to my first semester in college, and then took a semester off and went to Europe by myself. That was a good experience. I went for four months. I needed to do it. I proved to myself that I wasn't really alone, because I got as alone as you can be in a strange country and still found God there, everywhere.

What other word could I use for God? I was in Greece and a man almost hurt me because I wouldn't pay an extra toll. It was on a ship, and he dragged me all the way through it. People turned their backs and acted like nothing was happening until a family of Gypsies surrounded and protected me as he was ready to hit me.

Things like that make me believe.

Not that I'm so important that God will always step in to save me. I don't know. Everybody told me to be careful of the Gypsies, yet they were the ones who saved me.

There's something there. I don't presume to know more than anyone else. God can make people beautiful when you don't expect it.

Today, I'm a senior at Dominican University and trying my

best to be successful. I want to give things back, because I feel like I never had anything to give back before, and that makes me feel whole. I'm getting my B.A. in clinical and counseling psychology. I plan to go to graduate school to work with adolescents struggling with addictions.

I want to give back. My life is a gift, and I want to pass it along. It makes me happy to know there's a God, though it's unclear sometimes.

What's God? I have a hard time defining God, but it doesn't matter. How could I be expected to know? Who could be expected to know?

Like I said earlier, sometimes I *see* when I go to the oceans or just walk through the world. There are times, when I'm angry, when I feel it's all distant, that I blame God for things. Then I realize it's not God, but me. Who should I be blaming?

Spirituality is something you know. You feel it. It has nothing to do with the ordinary human stuff, the fear and pain that humans make easily enough.

The joy is so different. It could only come from somewhere else, from God that I love and strive for. I know this because there are times when I feel so weak. Then I want to give up. I know I can't. My life is the way it is today because of my belief and the work I've done and the people and the God I can't define who have been there for me. I know I can't just give up. I want to pass that on. You can do whatever you want if you work for it. I've been able to go after my dreams and do that.

I'm just so grateful.

I was nothing but a little girl crying in a bathtub, and everything hurt so much.

CHAPTER THIRTEEN

What's Left

IT'S AMAZING that we get through childhood at all. The emotions are huge and the information minimal. "Anyone who makes it through childhood has enough material to last a lifetime," Flannery O'Connor said.

We come into life saddled with genetic predispositions and enforced directions—the way the world is, the way our parents are, the voices saying how things should be, and families pretending to be families. "I'm just so grateful," Angela said. "I was . . . a little girl."

When a life can't break free it's pretty much a matter of genetic control. The weight of events, of the past decisions, gives an insistent push in the small of the back.

We remember the places where real things happened and cling to them, just as Angela thinks to herself, "Something must care for me." Such an astonishing judgment in a place of no hope.

We come into the world in love with the chambered warmth of a mother, but something goes wrong, there's nowhere to stop and rest, no safe place, and the eyes around are flat and angry. We make things up as best we can. We look up at a sky full of stars that clearly don't care but are so overpowering that a notion of implacability comes with them, and through the eyes. Maybe there's something else, too. Maybe it's nothing, but maybe it isn't.

This stirs us at the deepest level of perception. It's common in children to look outside. What do they find? What do we give them? We tell them, "This is how you grow up, by forgetting and ignoring." Mercifully, some can't forget, and keep trying.

Is there any hope? Sure, things can change. Everybody says so. How do things change?

There must be a key, but I don't have it. Angela had lost it as a little girl, and found it again.

Something is wrong with the world. If it were right, none of these things would have happened. What's wrong? Could *we* have been different? Then maybe *they* would have been different. At least I could have not cared and been someone else. At least I can still do that. I can be someone else. I just need something else.

Maybe if I'd had a father. What's a father like? It's a question Angela asked herself. "Well, he must know there's something wrong with me, and that's why he didn't want me, but a man who knows what's wrong could fix me if he wanted to. If I made him *like* me."

What's heartbreaking isn't the sudden disaster or the cataclysm. What's heartbreaking is the old photograph that shows us as we were. In it, we see *all* the children—hopeful, bright, and afraid.

The image of God as a father can be a terrible thing. Depending, of course, on who your father was.

How do the damaged fix themselves? That's what one imagines: to fix, as if there's a chemical that fixes things because they aren't right. You've been told that every child is loved, but when you look around, something isn't right, something or someone needs to be fixed.

At first, it's great that everything can come down to this

simple process—find a fix and use it. It gives direction to the day. Things seem to have a point. Maybe the fix is something mechanical, and we say, "I'll go to the same place every day and do the same thing and everything will be safe and all right." Maybe it's the flush of physical ecstasy when the crack hits. Maybe it's the satisfaction of having a gun in your hand when the bastards are scaring you. Maybe it's coming to a place where there are rules, and anyone who follows them will be safe and better than anyone who doesn't.

There are lots of pointless fixes short of giving up.

I went to see a lousy movie once, *Ironweed*, and it opened on an empty street with the bums waking up to the sunlight and stumbling out from cover, starting the day. I felt a terrible rush of loss. I couldn't do *that* anymore; I couldn't start a day with only one responsibility: to get something to drink.

I missed the certainty of it. I was astonished and frightened, and I hurt for every kind of loss there was, but as that faded I let the feelings sink in and rummage inside. It's odd that feelings can start at the surface and sink in, harmless at last.

And God is there in the aftermath! Nothing could tell you what's wrong, nothing to pass on the rules, to tell you how to avoid the pain. No limbs, face, booming voice, or manual to tell you how to eat, dress, or do your homework.

God, like a rose opening, blossoms in an understanding of love where there wasn't one before.

God comes when you give up, and giving up makes a space inside you for God. No more rationalizations, forgetting, and ignoring. No more mechanical guilt.

Love doesn't tell you what's wrong with you, either. Love doesn't make pain go away. It doesn't pick you up, carry you home, and put you to bed. Love is just there. You can hold on to it like a banister, like a strap in the subway, like a colored wooden bead on the side of your stroller. Angela knows that.

God is the final definition of the real. When the other stuff is gone, the real is what's left.

People arrive from all directions, and sometimes what gets them there is delusion, but because God is *the Real,* the first touch starts to clear the air of the mind.

❧

The next voice is Paul's. I grew up with him in Brooklyn.

Paul is in his fifties now. He lives in the Ojai Valley, in California, in a ranch-style house, airy, with a big backyard. He's married and has three remarkably likable children, quiet, bright, and amiable.

For a lot of reasons, he resists seeing his life as a story. We sit in the backyard at a patio table, under an umbrella, and talk about how things are. There's a big fertile yard in front of us, but with so many gopher holes, planting would be futile. There's a huge heron sitting in a tree at the far end. "He's the only gopher control that works at all," Paul says.

He has a big, sandy-haired head—Scots, French, and maybe Scandinavian—and a thick mustache that narrows into two dangling cords of hair like a modified Fu Manchu. He seems peaceful, at peace with who he is.

He did time in Vietnam, but the only reference he made to it was as "another scar on my soul."

He came to Ojai in the seventies so his kids could go to the Krishnamurti School. They were living in a school bus then, and a local came to their door one morning to tell him, "God made this valley for us to grow things in, not for people like you."

They might have said, "You were fit to die for us in Vietnam, but now you're not fit for much else." Their treatment of Paul reminds me of Sylvester in a Warner Brothers cartoon, Speedy Gonzalez and Sylvester. The mouse comes racing over snowy hills to a warm cabin with orange lights in the window. He knocks on the door and Sylvester answers. The mouse says, "Please, Señor, I am freezing and starving," and Sylvester says, "Of course you are. Rodents are supposed to freeze and starve."

Paul had a very serious heart operation about two years ago, but his peace now comes with no medical advice.

What you might not hear in the following is Paul's marvelous wit. I remember he asked me once what I was doing on the Internet. I said, "I'm researching fourteenth-century Eskimo pornography."

"Look under 'Popsicles,'" he said.

So here's Paul's story, told in a brief conversation in front of the rolling green valley and the eyes of the enormous heron.

CHAPTER FOURTEEN

Paul

BEFORE I WENT into the service, I did religious stuff like going to church on Sunday, and the youth fellowship program. Things like that. But there was always something missing because none of it was spiritual. It was a religious thing. You know what that was like. I mean if you think about the building and all the churchgoers and their kids and how they were, you know there wasn't much you could call spiritual.

After military service in Korea and Vietnam, I just gave up completely on the church. It seemed like so much bullshit. After that time I started drinking heavily. I didn't think I was an alcoholic, but that didn't matter, because I was drunk all the time and aimless. I had no direction. I was just like a weed, blowing here and blowing there.

Two bars to a block on Third Avenue.

Sometimes three. But after Trish and I were married and came back from New Zealand, a friend gave me Ouspensky's *The Fourth Way* to read. I'd been looking around, but when I read Ouspensky I became conscious of *mechanicalness.* There's repetition and brutality in mechanical states, and it made sense. I could fit it in to what I'd seen.

I went to the Art Students League to study painting. While I was there, I was exposed to the works of Krishnamurti. It was funny, because the point was to read them as an approach to painting, and I did. The more I read, the more they went into my life, and then into the paintings, and then back again.

So it was all one loop.

It was at this point that I realized that *religion* was different from what many would call *spiritual*. I would say that "spiritual" is really being in touch with what is.

I think we can come to things by accident—when we take things away, or things are taken away, we get to see what's left and shift out of the mechanical.

Yeah. You think you have a story, and it makes sense. When you start to see it as mechanical, when you even suspect it's nothing but that, something explodes and strips the story bare, and you're nowhere.

I was lost. Just aimless.

When I was growing up I was trapped inside stories, and they were terrible. My grandfather Gus was always down in the big furnace room, taking care of it because it was always fucking up.

There was a corner down there, next to the furnace, and if you looked with a flashlight you'd see thousands of water bugs in the dark, crawling all over each other.

God, yes. I remember one day he took me with him. A cat was down there and fighting with something, maybe rats, and was torn up so bad you wouldn't believe it. One eye was just hanging by a cord. It was terrible, but my grandfather just opened the furnace, scooped him up on a shovel, and threw him in. I was just standing there, watching, trying to understand. That comes out of the other stuff. It meant something. I probably didn't want to know what it meant, so it just stayed in my head till I could deal with it.

All the time I'm going to church and I'm supposed to believe and my grandfather is part of all that. He's a grown-up and knows, or he's supposed to know. So what was there to know?

The biggest part of going to church, as far as I could tell, was wearing a suit and jingling change in your pocket. Taps, too, clicking your taps on the sidewalk. I was always embarrassed about not going to church. It was like I was afraid they'd find out we were different.

I didn't have to worry about that because we were going on Sundays, but I didn't have any reason to believe or not believe. Things happening in my life that were a lot realer than anything I heard in church. Like I said about the furnace thing, some things stick and don't go away. There's some reason to pay attention to them.

One Sunday, Robby, Mr. Clancy's son, came out the front doors with a puppy on a leash. I was the only one around, and I bent down to pet him. Robby said, "Don't touch him. My dad said not to let anyone touch him." I patted him on the head anyway.

That night Robby comes down and says his father wants to see me. So I go up there and the old man says, "I want you to see this because it's your fault." He makes Robby take his pants down and lie on the couch so he can beat him with his belt. I went back downstairs in a daze.

You told me that once before. You called it "Another scar on my soul."

I don't remember ever saying that, let alone twice.

You said it.

Huh, okay. I don't remember. But I know what you're talking about. The problem lies in our mechanicalness, conditioning, and our psychological memory. Our lives are stories lived in our heads and acted out on a stage. Remembering that none of it is actually real can lead to "being," or at least partial insight.

I understand when you say you don't have anything to say about God because there's nothing you could say about him. I come at it from a different angle, maybe, but I understand that belief is nothing, a mental process, and that most of the brutality attached to religion is a matter of belief. It permits it and fills the head with a lot of doubtful stuff.

It's like when I hear "Higher Power" I think, "What does that mean? Is there a lower power? Is there a power above higher?" At some point it means nothing to me, and if it means nothing I can't deal with it, because I'm not willing to be mechanical. I know what that does. I've been there.

There's a point, though, a place, where there's just the feeling of having been touched. Then things are never quite the same. I mean I watch you here and I know you've been touched. I can feel it.

There's a better place to be than where I was. I'll say that.

Is it a place?

It isn't anything. I don't have a name.

Neither do I, but I use the shorthand.

Yeah. It's like I said, I don't believe there's a Higher Power because I don't believe there's a lower power. I don't believe we have any power at all, or that there's a conscious power to talk about, as if God did this or that and here are the reasons. I don't believe in power or that we have any. Nor should we. Nor does anything or anybody else. None of my kids was born with an instruction manual. All the different countries and cultures have different explanations and Gods and ideals. Who knows? Nobody knows.

If I have to assume that I know, I'm fucked.

When I was a kid going to church, all that Jesus, God, heaven, and hell stuff were very real, as real as Santa Claus for a kid. Religion and spirituality were fused together. They were the same thing.

After Nam they weren't. I had a lot of guilt about Nam. Close friends were being killed. Back in the States, I saw all that bullshit on TV. These guys on television in Vietnam I had been with a week before. The war made less sense every day. Our government betrayed us. I threw the church and the state out the window.

I went to Australia and then New Zealand for ten years to get away from it all. But no matter where I went, there I was.

For me it was good to begin to see things in terms of mechanical being, mechanical response, because out of that comes right action that is free from the known and the mechanicalness.

When I was about ten, I rode my bike with another kid down by Nelly Bly and saw the pony ride. It cost fifty cents to go around the track twice. We only had fifty cents between us, so I asked the guy if we could each go around once. Of course he agreed, so around we went. After the first go-round, I got the pony back to the stalls, but it was hard. It had been going around the circle twice for such a long time, it took great effort to move the pony from its appointed rounds. I saw my friend going around automatically for the second time. He couldn't stop the pony. I was sure that we would be in trouble.

For years I thought about how conditioned the pony had been and how unfair it was that my friend got to go around twice without punishment. Many years later, I realized that I was every bit as conditioned as the pony. I could no more have gone around the circle twice than fly, even though the pony wanted to and the guy didn't care. Why?

The threat of an unknown and dreadful punishment was hanging over my head.

God? Mother? Santa?

The stuff with the cat and old man Clancy were shocks.

They were part of the unimaginable and unpredictable events that shocked me into awareness and out of the dream of the story that we are. Unfortunately, they became another story, and that one was aimlessness for a long time.

About the best advice I ever got came from Sergeant Watson in Nam, who told me, "Don't believe anything you hear, and only half of what you see." Man, was he ever right.

If only we believed in what we *don't* know. God has nothing to do with religion, spirituality, or anything like that. It's beyond words and thoughts. You can't go to it or use it. It or God comes to the "not you." It's idiotic to think that when you die all your thought baggage stays in the one place. All that baggage is the false you.

I went to the doctor because I wasn't feeling good. They practically wheeled me to the OR from his office. I had very little time. Everything was clogged around my heart and the arteries had to be cleared. Right away. I had little time to think. I knew that where I was, was not the place I wanted to be.

Well, it was a strange thing. I was in a place where I didn't really matter. It was out of my hands. I had this knowing that I was dying, and the realization that it was out of my hands seemed to make the world very quiet and peaceful.

It took a bit to accept, but when I did, the world became quiet. I returned home with that peace, which was a good thing. Had the doctors not intervened, you'd be channeling this interview.

What about your life, day to day?

Oh, my children are the most important to me. They're the future. I've always wanted them to (I've always *invited* them to) see the world through their own eyes, how they are a part of it, and not apart. I encourage them to try to see things as they are, which is what you'd probably call a spiritual discipline. Once you see the mechanical, you just don't want to be there anymore.

Is there a direction? Do you feel like you're moving one way or another?

I don't know. The poet E. E. Cummings says it pretty well. He wrote:

> seeker of truth
> follow no path
> all paths lead where
> truth is here

To be really simple about it, I'd ask, "Why on earth would a god take a personal interest in me? Isn't it always the other way around?" I try to laugh as much as I can. You know the joke about the Buddha in New York?

No.

What did the Buddha say to the hot dog vendor?

What?

"Make me one with everything."

It all depends on whether I'm in a mechanical state or not. If I am, then there I am with the gopher out of *Caddyshack.*

If not, not there at all, there's just an immense beauty frozen in time.

You want to stop now?

Oh, you know . . . thinking about things, it doesn't stop.

CHAPTER FIFTEEN

All of This Goes Where?

THE APARTMENT BUILDING where Paul and I grew up in New York was a big, strange place. It took up a lot of the block. It was six stories high and had two wings arranged around a central courtyard with stone benches, stone lions, and cypress hedges. There were probably ten to fifteen kids in the place. The number varied as families moved to the suburbs. This was after World War II, though we weren't baby boomers. We were born during the war and remembered.

I always had a sense of something unusual about the place, the Fleetwood, as it was called. A few years ago, I went back and looked up kids I'd known. I'd written a book about those years, a book with a lot of intuitive jumps into other kids' heads and an overriding concern with God and poetry as they exist in the child's world.

The ones I found and talked to said, "Yeah, it was just like that." Which was remarkable because all I'd done was take *my* memories of emotions and spread them across all of us: the earliest shocks of the sky and the stars, the sense of the world as a swirl of unknown adult codes, not being sure in the mornings and stepping out into the backyard. There was more: the deep astonishments of beauty and geography, the map of the streets and their deeper and shallower stretches, the confusion about church and how God was there and wasn't, the sense that each of us was a secret in our families and couldn't let out the sadness or the confusion.

There were usually five girls in our crowd. Three of them became nuns. They promised each other when they were ten or so and kept their promises.

We were oddly isolated. We didn't have much to do with kids from other buildings. We were innocent, I think, compared with the run of the neighborhood kids.

I remember Paul's eyes, woundlike, when we were growing up. He seemed right on the edge of tears. I was, too, but I had a will of iron, and no one was going to see my tears. Paul was open to being hurt, and a kid like that scares all the others. "What if he were me?" It was good he was there to remind us of the real.

All of this goes where? I don't know.

I remember us on the roof in the summer night, watching the fireworks over Coney Island. The younger we were, the quieter we were. There were nights we peered through a little telescope, looking at the stars and matching constellations to the drawings in a book. We weren't allowed on the roof, but it was a place at night that opened into mystery.

I never sensed that there wasn't one of us who didn't respond to the great dark empty bowl and the run of the stars. There were more stars to see then. The air was cleaner and the ambient light negligible.

On the roof, we were friends, more or less, under a huge mystery. Like all kids, we took the mystery as it was and tried to understand. In our beds in the dark, we had dreams, and while we never told each other what they were, we could see them in the others' eyes. We never talked about our families, either, especially the kids who had to deal with chaos and terror. Yet, we could see, we could see it in their eyes.

On summer nights, we'd gather fireflies in huge jars, then set them down and quietly watch the life blinking in the soft twilight.

We were more like each other than we were different. I think *that's* where this is going. Gradually, as we grew and scattered, we came to think we were isolated quantities and not much alike at all.

So when I sat and talked to Paul or went back to the Fleetwood to talk to Carol and to Barbara, I went back to the heart of things. Sure enough, we were more alike than not. Every remembered grouping, every night on the roof under fireworks, was like a choir, as if we'd been gathered together to pray inarticulately.

Which was what we were doing, as a matter of fact. Each of us in the dark was sure there was something out there. We each dealt with it, trying because we hadn't learned to lie in our heads yet.

I know because I asked, and because Paul, sitting in his gopher-pocked yard in Ojai, remembered the same things, and the same vastnesses.

❧

That mystery and vastness leads me to Pat, an Irish Catholic from Queens. She's five foot four or so, with red hair and bright eyes. She likes to laugh and has a good one, easy and musical.

She must have been a rare, rare beauty, a John Ford heroine, because when I met her she was in her sixties and still beautiful, with agreeable traces of what they used to call a hot number.

She's been sober for a long time, thirty-seven years. Before she retired, she'd spent the previous twenty-five years working in treatment. She isn't particularly well right now and needs transfusions on a monthly basis, but there's still more life in her voice than you'll hear in any random sampling of twenty-year-olds.

She's instinctively reticent, but always manages to say what she means. She has a lot of children and grandchildren. Most of them come by to see her.

She once said that the reason she never had a drink again after starting in AA was that she thought she wasn't allowed to.

Pat is a delight, though her eyes have an occasional, powerful charge of loss and general sadness. She has a slightly spoiled dog.

CHAPTER SIXTEEN

Pat

OKAY, I'M PATRICIA, and I have this whole story in my head, if I can only get it out.

I'm going to start with an incident that happened to me when I was very young, probably about six or seven, maybe eight. This was in the time of the depression, in the early 1930s or thereabouts. Although most people we knew, and in fact the whole country, were not doing very well financially (and it was affecting them in many ways), my dad was doing quite well.

He was a policeman with a steady job and benefits, such as they had in those days. He was making money, very good money. We were living well during the depression. We were able to rent a bungalow in Rockaway Beach on Long Island from the middle of June to the middle of September every year for a number of years. I think it cost us $175 for that whole time. It was pretty nice. Looking back on it from the perspective of age, it turned out to be the grace in the chaos that was all around my family.

I always looked forward to going to the bungalow. I remember it from my early years. I couldn't articulate how I felt, even now I can't, but, looking back, I see that place as a spiritual one.

On some levels, I didn't and don't understand that at all. On another level, I think I do. Every morning I would wake up very early. The sun was up. I'd put on my swimsuit, grab a piece of bread or piece of toast, and walk down to the beach. The beach was about two or three blocks from where we were living. I would go down there, as I said, very early, about 6:30 A.M.

I'd run and throw myself in the sand and revel in the whole world of sand and the ocean and the sky and the sun. I had this feeling of being complete and being free, at least for that moment.

I'd spend two hours or so down at the beach by myself. Sometimes somebody else would walk by, but nobody ever spoke. We nodded, acknowledged each other's presence, but we were in our own places and didn't want to break that.

Eventually, my mother found out I was going to the beach every morning. She extracted a promise from me that I would not go swimming, because I wasn't allowed to swim without a grown-up there. I think I kept that promise. It wasn't about swimming anyway. It was just about *being there,* going there. The world was all mine before most people were awake.

I would do all kinds of things. I'd run and collapse in the sand. I'd search for sea shells and oddities. I'd build huge sand castles with tunnels and everything. I knew some boy would come along and jump on it, destroy it, but that was okay because I could make another one.

Sometimes I would just sit on the beach and look out at the horizon—it seemed to me the horizon of the morning—and the ocean. I've always loved the ocean. I don't know what kind of thoughts I had. I do remember what a wonderful thing I was doing. I felt, without being able to describe it as a child, that somehow I was suspended in time. Maybe we'd call it transcendence. I felt that as a child.

Even though I had to go back to the bungalow, for that little bit of time, the ocean and beach belonged to me. When I'd walk home, probably around eight in the morning, I saw little cafés as I walked across the boardwalk. Most all of them were owned and run by Japanese.

After a while, the owners got used to seeing me walking back and forth. They looked after me. They talked to me and got to know me. They had trouble pronouncing my name so they'd call me "Girlie."

One man would say, "Oh! I see you coming. I see you coming, I make you an egg sandwich." He would hold out a paper plate with an egg sandwich on it. Another would say, "Oh, you need milk. Need milk, here drink your milk." I'd have to drink my milk while he stood there and watched. Sometimes I'd hear, "You stay too long today. You stay too long. We worry about you."

I never did know any of their names, but I knew as a child that these men were just nice. These days it would carry some edge of sex or potential abuse, but it wasn't that way at all. They were kind, loving people. I looked forward to seeing them. They were part of the mornings and going to the beach. I remember I was at the beach in 1939 when the war between England and Germany was declared. In 1941, all the Japanese men were gone. I never saw them again.

I guess they were already putting them in the camps. I never heard about the camps until I came to San Francisco in 1946. I thought it was terrible and realized, "That's where those men probably went." Afterward, I always felt something incomplete at the beach. I've thought about them through my life as kind, gentle men. They were part of the one special place in my life, which was the beach and its world. Maybe there's some completion in just thinking about them over and over. It's hard to say or understand.

I told this story first because the beach has a very special place in my heart and life. The beach was the saving grace of my child-hood. It was an image of grace. Those images never go away.

In my home, alcoholism, unresolved issues, and chaos were a big part of my childhood. Outside, everything was different. There were so many kids. I never see kids at all around here, but in those days in the city, the streets were full of kids playing, es-pecially in the summer. Now parents and kids are frightened. Then we'd play ring-a-levio. Even kids who didn't like each other would strike a truce to play ring-a-levio. During my childhood, I actually had a lot of fun—out of the house.

We used to go ice skating in the winter when they'd freeze over the tennis courts. We'd go sledding. They had some great hills in the park.

There was a kid in my class named Dorothea. I'll never for-get her. We had assembly every week and had to get dressed up. We noticed in assembly that Dorothea didn't salute the flag. Kids started getting upset about this, and would poke her: "Do this, do that." The teachers didn't seem to catch on. One day after school (this was a big school) there was some kind of con-frontation. Somebody was yelling at Dorothea. I was coming down the steps and saw her, trying to defend herself.

There was something strange about being a Jehovah's Wit-ness. They didn't salute the flag. It was a mob scene; they were pushing her all over the place.

I was shouting in the beginning like everybody else. Then I got scared, because I didn't know what was going to happen. Dorothea had a brother who ran home and told their father. He came down. He was a big man, probably six feet tall, and jumped into the middle, yelling. All the kids went away, of course.

What happened to her was the opposite of spiritual. I re-member the feeling now, and it's empty. How easily we could have hurt that little girl. I guess there was *something* there, because if there wasn't, why did I hate the way I did? Why do I remember it now?

These are the strong memories of my childhood, when I think about who I was and where God might have been.

I was sent to church and catechism, confirmation, but I never quite believed in the Catholic church. I grew up semibelieving, not thinking much about it. I married my first husband in a courthouse in Jamaica, and my mother of course would not acknowledge our marriage because we didn't marry in the church. Not until we did could she say, "Well, congratulations."

Nevertheless, I was imbued with the importance of having religion. Later I went to church sporadically. When the kids started coming along, I sent them, the way my mother had. My sense of a spiritual life was practically nil, I can tell you that.

Alcohol made me change.

I'd been drinking for years. I didn't realize that I was an alcoholic. I knew I had a small drinking problem, but I was too much of a nice Catholic girl, I guess, to be an alcoholic. I was a mother and wife, so I couldn't possibly be alcoholic.

I had one child, then another, a little boy. When he was sixteen months old, he got spinal meningitis and died in the night. It's something I find very hard to talk about. It never goes away. We never forget that.

I had already begun to drink alcoholically at that point. After the child died—his name was Brian—my husband and I grew apart.

It's so strange to me. Yet, I've seen it happen many times in my life. When a tragedy occurs, it doesn't bring people closer together. It just makes for division. You grieve, but not together. I can't explain it. I've never really tried to figure it out. But

Brian's death was a deep, deep hurt that has lasted till now. I still feel it.

When I went on a Saint Patrick's Day drunk, I came out of a blackout, late at night, to find myself in an unsavory place. In AA, they'll talk about having "a moment of clarity." I had that and thought, "My God, what am I doing here?" It was a bar in the Mission in San Francisco, skid row, really. There were faces around me, and the wet kind of feel and smell.

For the next few days I stopped drinking. It took a while before I began to feel well again. I'd not had a drink for four or five days and went to a friend's house because I knew she always had booze. At her house, we had two sixteen-ounce cans of beer.

While I was sitting with her, something terrible was happening inside me. I felt nothing but remorse and despair. My friend said, "Come on. Open up another beer, and to hell with it. Let's have another drink." So we opened this beer, and I held it in my hand. I was looking down at it.

I thought, "You know what? If you drink this drink, you don't know where you're gonna wind up. The last time was a terrible place, and this next time could be worse." I looked down at the beer for what seemed like eternity (the same kind of eternity as on the beach when the whole world came around for me and stopped). Then something happened, like a shift in my being. Everything I had been and all the things I had stored up in me, the chaos, the drunkenness, and the little girl watching, came forward. I had some real strength, but it was all wrapped up in a desire to kill the pain at all costs. Suddenly that afternoon something inside me shifted. Maybe I could *see* beyond all the jumble. I didn't want the beer. I put it down, got up, went home, and called AA.

It might have happened other times. I remember once coming out of a blackout on the way down a very steep hill on a bi-cycle with a bottle in my hand. However, that wasn't the one that did it.

Maybe three touches of God is all a life needs.

Maybe all a life needs is one experience in childhood that says, "This is the world and it's beautiful, and it's mine and this is who I always want to be." Maybe that's enough to break through and make you see that the world that could have been still is. When I started sobriety, the first thing that came to my mind was the beach, that sense of time that wasn't time, or some kind of watching from somewhere else.

I decided to stop. My body was saturated with alcohol, and it didn't take very much. My kids were great. They tried to help me, made me coffee, and I went to my first meeting that night.

I was shaking when a very nice woman and her husband came to pick me up for the meeting. The woman said to me, "Well, Pat, if you're really sick, maybe you shouldn't go. We could let you rest and take you another time."

"No, no," I said. I knew that if I stayed home I wouldn't get to another meeting.

At the meeting, there was a round table. I had gotten sick before the meeting. I was looking around and seeing these people who were nicely dressed. The women had their hair done. My hair was a mess. I thought, "Oh, they can't possibly want me around here."

When they got to me (it was one of those moments of spirit), I raised my hand and said I was an alcoholic. They all started clapping. As the meeting went on, I stayed sick, but I was in a place where I could absorb stuff without really thinking about it. It was a feeling of coming home. I had never felt so comfort-able so quickly in any place before.

I left that meeting that night feeling ecstatic. I felt there was hope for me, "a wretch like me." That's how I was thinking. I got sick again after the meeting, but went home feeling that I'd found something. I didn't want to let it go. That's where I really found spirituality.

The way was not easy. It was very difficult to stay sober, a battle I fought every day. Many people say that when they join AA the urge to drink leaves them, but that wasn't the case with me. It took quite a long time, but I stayed with it. As they used to say, "No matter what happens, don't drink. No matter what." I didn't.

I had married again, but my second husband died about a year later. Then there was an AA marriage. That was a disaster. I knew almost right away that he wasn't for me. I wasn't in love with him. I didn't even really like him all that much. I had no idea. Why I even agreed to marry him is a mystery to me.

Understand that I didn't get smart or injury-proof through a Higher Power. I didn't get buckets of money or the key to success. What I got was a measure of peace and strength.

When I married this man in AA, we had a child, a little boy, Kevin. Kevin was four months old when he died of spinal meningitis. I couldn't believe it could happen to me again. In fact, I went through a time when I thought I was cursed.

My brother had been killed in 1945 in the Philippines. Then my son Brian died, then my mother, my father, my husband, and then Kevin. I didn't want to get close to anybody, because I believed I would pass on the curse. I remember thinking it wasn't fair. It wasn't. I had struggled to get sober. I did get sober, and this happened again. I couldn't believe it.

The day of the baby's funeral, people came, and more people, but after all that I found myself pacing a long hallway in my house. I smoked cigarette after cigarette. I was beside myself. I felt like a tiger coiled up and ready to spring. At the slightest provocation, I'd spring.

I called a friend and went to a meeting in an auditorium in Richmond. It was a huge auditorium filled with a thousand people or so. I sat next to my friend and felt distant from anything the speaker said. I couldn't hear him. I felt enclosed in a glass sphere of some kind. I could look out and see people. I could hear them, but their sounds were muted.

I was isolated and cold in this glass bubble. I was planning how I would get drunk the next day. I was planning what kind of alcohol I would drink. What would I do with my children? Send them to the movies? I'd get whiskey and just drink it down. That was all I wanted.

The speaker was finishing and said, "We came to believe." When he said that, I felt electricity or what I perceived as electricity go through me. Suddenly, it was as though the glass wall had gone away and I was alive again. I realized I did not want to get drunk. I did not want to get drunk tomorrow. I sat there, not meditating, but letting the feeling wash over me.

That's what it is. It isn't a thought or an insight, but a wave and it moves into you. I didn't get drunk the next day. I still had seven children alive and well. They needed me.

I had five teenagers. I had to do a lot of praying, letting go, and paying attention. One of the great things about having a discipline like AA is that it gives you an opportunity to explore spirituality or to place yourself in a position where spiritual things can happen to you more easily. Not that they can't happen to anyone. AA people have no monopoly on that, though I think we've been put in a place where we're more open.

We never had enough money, but life went on. Eventually

my children got older, and life got easier. I found a good job. From that time until a few years ago, I worked all through life. I did some things that might be called touchy-feely. That helped. When you open your heart you get vulnerable, but somewhere along the way, if you're lucky, you learn some common sense.

I worked at an insurance company for a while, but they lost a bunch of contracts and laid off about fifteen hundred people. I could have gotten a job elsewhere in the company, but I didn't like them very much and thought they lacked integrity. I wanted to try something new, so I took my severance pay and went on a two-week walking trip in Greece. Athens was at the end of a fifty-mile or so walk. I had one of the best times of my life. I was proud because I'd gone by myself.

There was another marriage. He was a persistent guy who just wore me down. It wasn't good. After it was over, I rallied myself. I saw Ray on Friday night, Jack on Saturday night, Tom on Sunday night, and one other who just bought me dinner. It was a really nice time and I felt cared for, loved, and of course, things finally leveled out.

I sold my house and moved to Oakland to be with another jerk. I mean I just didn't have good taste in men. Then there was a man whom I'd known for a long time. He was seventeen years younger than me, but one night he made a pass at me at the club. We started going out. That shocked the pants off everyone, especially my ex-husband.

David finally moved in with me, and we were together for about a year. We had a great time. We put on a couple of plays. We took classes at the music conservatory. One night, we listened to Vaughan Williams's *A Lark Ascending,* and it was so absolutely exquisite that at the end we were holding hands with tears streaming down our faces. There were so many emotions in it. It was another place entirely, almost a meditative place.

It took me years to be able to sit down and meditate. I do it now, but I won't lie and say I do it every day. I do it as often as I can, because it can put you in another state.

Learning how to let go of things that are no longer important in your life comes with aging, the "years," but a lot of them have been like lead. It's very hard at times to maintain my serenity. Because of my health problems, it's hard not to get depressed.

It's stressful. I found, not exactly a solution, but a way to deal with stress and anxiety. I was feeling that way last week when I met this guy at a meeting, and he said, "Hi, Pat, how are you doing?" I just started to cry.

I don't know where it came from, but it worked.

Sometimes I'll just let myself be ill. I might give it a time limit. I think, "Okay, you can whine and moan and mope around and carry on for a day or two, but that's it." Basically, that's what I do. Right now I try to meditate every day, though I don't always succeed.

My relationship with four of my daughters is excellent. My oldest son, who lives next door, is good to me in his own way. My youngest son isn't part of the family anymore. I don't know why. He just removed himself. I guess I just have to let him live his own way.

My daughter Sue is still mad at me for something that happened five years ago. She was having her own problems with drugs and was neglecting her children at that time. I blew the whistle, and she's never forgiven me.

I don't have a whole lot more to say, but I'd like to explain that my life today is good and that I need to live in the now.

When I wake up every morning, I feel good to be here. So

I'm glad to talk about these things. It's a chance for me to reflect on what's been good in my life, and how it showed itself to me early on. One good thing about getting older is you don't have to be defensive. You can get away with stuff, and I like that.

I'm on good terms with most people in my life (if *they* could just get their acts together, we could be much happier). I'm usually the oldest person at a meeting, in terms of age and sobriety (thirty-seven years).

If I had to pick something recent, something from my adult years that is important or clear as to how things are for me, how I see things, and what God is to me, I'd probably pick a day about fifteen years ago. Things were going pretty well then. I was driving through Golden Gate Park. It was about five o'clock on a kind of balmy day. I was listening to Mozart, driving, when everything that was or is came together in an instant that could have been forever. I felt pure joy.

God, I was glad to be alive. I remember it perfectly and can touch the feeling sometimes. Now, that's something.

CHAPTER SEVENTEEN

Moments of Loveliness

I WORKED WITH PAT in treatment. It was in an old ramshackle building with about twenty rooms. Every day there were two three-hour, intense groups. Most of the residents had come to the absolute end of the road, with nothing left but to live or die. Neither was going to be easy.

There were four of us working as counselors. The other three were Harry, whom I've mentioned; Dave, a looming, frightening guy who'd missed gentleness in his life and worked at it; and Pat. Pat had been hired because when she sat in the group room for an interview, she'd had little or nothing to say but projected perfect attention. She was a bright-eyed mix of inquisitiveness and defiance. All of us were recovering, so she fit right in with her twenty-odd years of sobriety. That's when she told us that she'd stayed sober in AA only because she'd thought that if she drank she'd be asked to leave.

She was petite, lovely, and hard as nails about how you stay sober. Her whole past was available to her and others, which is important in recovery because it lets everyone else know that nothing is off limits and that all lives will become whole and manageable at the point of surrender.

I made a free-form shrine for her one morning. I guess it was for her birthday The shrine was all wires and things and photographs and bits of paper. At the base was a typed square that said, "For Patricia T., Erected this 7th of December by her Dazed Ex-husbands and Their Psychiatric Social Workers."

She laughed with real delight. She's always been able to turn suddenly into a laughing little girl. The girl in her meditation, running and running to get to the beach where she'd be alone with the planet and emptied time, is as real to me as those substantial, intense days in the old house.

I read a piece once that said, mysteriously, that alcoholics have abnormalities in the memory control center. The what? It was the kind of offhand, unclear nonsense that one expects in the daily papers, but it rattled around in my head for a long time. I don't know any drunks who don't have instants of total recall—set pieces in their minds that come back unwilled, at odd times. Some are moments of loveliness, as if a child were being given something to hold on to for a lifetime.

I come back to that specific sense of memory that holds a life together till one or two or three memories are understood and opened. What haunts me is that many never get to that place where they open, and there's a sudden understanding that can't be understood. So I think, "Pay attention to the odd things, the broken moments, the sudden knowledge that comes from nowhere, the dream with the meat and density of the real, the fugitive wholeness, the slant of light on the carpet that stops the mind, the déjà vu bells ringing, the wild accesses to joy, and the overpowering instant of 'this is more real than everything else.'"

It all glimmers and vibrates and points and brings with it the way we were and the way we saw in another time. Buried in the seeing is the secret that the person seeing then, no matter how far back, is the same person seeing now. It's feelable, the eyes in the head knowing nothing but watching the same way as right now—the other, the real thing, the lost murmuring soul in perpetuity.

Remember? Before the depredations of event and personality and social necessity? Remember the pair of eyes and the voice in the head? If you go back as far as you can, if you find an instant out of time, can you remember the heart of how you were? Did you want bad things to happen to people? Did you want the world to be cheap and cruel? Did you want the brutal, or did it stun you and cause you fear and grief? Cause *us* fear and grief.

Where do we go? "Where can I go without you?" as the song has it.

See the little girl down on the beach in the morning sun. They're all looking at her, but where is she? You can't disappear, not really. But there's a level of nonrecognition that's close to having disappeared. Where have you, the child, gone? Who knows the child anymore? The mind splits a little, grieving and uncomprehending, and when the space is made, love fills it and everything rises up to be accessible again. Dispassionately, the old voice murmurs and the bright eyes see. "In all the old familiar places . . ."

If you want to be alive, go to the places where people are trying to be honest: the one-time hunting lodge with the dark corners, the windows on the steep street, or the eyes shining like battered, living marbles. That's where God is, too. I've looked around the churches plenty of times, but never felt him quite the way I did in a roomful of people having to care for each other because if they didn't, they were doomed. They'd all come to the point of God, which is the place where the personality falls apart like a Tinkertoy, and the moments of grace, however few, have a sudden life of their own and ring softly in the dark.

I've thanked God (not a person or big draped thing in the sky) for alcohol, when I realized how efficient it had been in breaking me down to a level of grace (twenty-three years is nothing). Then I'd remember, just as suddenly, what I'd done to other people and shrink from my self-centeredness. Vanity is a horrible thing, and made of vicious loneliness.

The opposite of vanity is truth. There can be moments when the world swirls around and stops. There isn't anything that matters, because you can feel endless forgiveness and the certainty of love in every seam, every crack of existence. It comes most readily when the personality has come to hate the wounded soul and the personality structure, so unstable that the lies begin to topple it. It comes when the false notions of strength and the noxious vanities are gone. The mind gives up and floats, astonished.

People everywhere can say what to do in order to get where they are. The problem is that they tell us to let go, and everything we've learned says, "No, I can't do that."

I heard a guy in a group say, "I don't know how to tell the truth."

"Stop lying," Dave said. We bring ourselves to a place where there's a hideous space between who we were and wanted to be and what we've become.

The space can fill up with substance, if we let it. It isn't a matter of finding God. God is always there. God is the substance. It's just a matter of paying attention until something breaks and makes a space. It's a matter of God inside coming to rest in the God that seemed to be outside.

❧

It's the light in Pat's eyes. Don is next, with a wonderfully different voice, the matter-of-fact voice of someone who sees everything with a level of astonishment. He has come to play it down because he knows his words aren't up to it anyway, nor are anyone else's. He remembers a time when "believe or not believe" meant something. His mind then was up to the distinction.

Now he deals with a world of inexplicability. Everything is inexplicable in its own way. For him, a fabric of things exists and events link in a great, barely moving wave.

I've seen Don around for years and heard him speak. His manner is a brief and practical guide to saying what can be said while honoring the unsayable. He's a little owlish, though his face is long rather than full. He talks sometimes with his arms folded, resisting the expressiveness of the hands, about which he would have to know a great deal.

CHAPTER EIGHTEEN

Don

I WAS ASKED by the authors of this book to relate my experience in coming to some sort of spiritual awakening. I don't mean to engage in any parlor psychiatry or to analyze myself, but just say how I see things. If it should be of use, I'm glad to share it.

My beginnings were in California in 1940. I was raised in northern California. I was the last of four children, and our parents were both deaf-mute people, which made our family somewhat unique because of the sign language and the attention it brought us in public. I noticed people looking at us at a very young age, and I was immediately ashamed.

I guess like most children I found my security, love, and sense of family with Mama. I remember clutching Mama's leg for security and feeling all would be well.

I don't know if my neighborhood was any rougher than others, but we kids were pretty harsh on each other. There were so many differences between us culturally, and it was easy to pick out those differences and make fun of each other. We got negative verbal skills.

The attacks I got were mostly about my parents and about my being small and having big ears. I suppose they were positive in some sense, because rough things early on like that can put hide on you. But for me, it didn't work that way. I got very insecure. So what I did to defend myself was to get good at throwing verbal barbs. I didn't have brawn, so I had to have mental speed and agility. I was good on the streets until I was about fifteen, when we moved away and into the "normal white kids" neighborhood.

I expected the same in that neighborhood, but those kids didn't have the verbal skills I had. I was *very* good, and their abuse wasn't as polished as mine. I felt pretty secure that no one would make fun of me. I hate to think of myself now as good at verbal assault, but that's what I was.

I noticed right away that the new kids were dressed better and had better lunch boxes, and I began to feel inadequate about that. We were poor. In junior high and high school, some of my friends could buy cars. They had houses, too.

We had always been apartment dwellers—users and borrowers. I wasn't used to being around people who had their own places. I tried to use self-reliance to bolster myself so I could feel comfortable with my peers. Some kids had beauty, brawn, or intelligence—my gift was personality.

I was good at schmoozing and was well liked. When necessary, I could defend myself verbally. I was a social animal and felt pretty comfortable around people. My social skills helped me to feel secure.

Around the age of sixteen, I took my first drink of alcohol. I liked it. I liked the effect of it. I took it as often as I could. During that summer, I had my first drink and got drunk. Since I didn't have classes or a job, I was into all-night drinking that summer. I liked what alcohol did for me. I liked the fact that it made me feel secure in my own skin. I could let my hair down. I didn't have to be aware anymore of what was going on around me so I could be ready for a threat. I let go and I let booze.

By this time I was in high school. I didn't come from a

family that encouraged me in school. We were just left on our own. My folks were not making sure I did my homework. I was pretty self-willed anyway through adolescence, with all that that implies.

In school, I was a good-time Charlie. I was underdressed, had no money, no car, and felt inadequate, but I was using my personality full-time, trying to meet girls.

Scholastically I wasn't good. I didn't like discipline, regular commitments, or homework. I couldn't put all the parts of studying together. The parts consisted of getting a chair, a light, a table, a book, and a chapter: the elements of study. I was starting to become completely self-willed and oddly antisocial, considering my skills for socializing. I thought it was better to go my own way while being popular.

To be popular was *the* big thing. I guess in my time the term was "cool." As I remember, the cool kids in school were the ones who didn't carry books, who smoked, and who did their own thing. I avoided tests and assignments and didn't focus or look down the road or think about vocation or anything else. I was a rudderless ship.

Being that way and being self-willed, I didn't take advice or guidance from anyone. I rebelled against all that. With this self-willed approach to the world (what had got me to where I was), I threw away my education.

After graduating from high school, I went to work and escalated my drinking.

I was drinking whenever I could. I was young, and it was still a good time. I worked for a summer at a well-known clothing store in San Francisco, where I was introduced to dressing properly for the first time. I got my clothing for nothing.

My boss was a good man who got me back into school, City

College of San Francisco. I still had no idea what to do vocationally, so I pulled toward the fraternity scene. I became a big man on campus, Freddy Frat-Rat, all that crap.

I had a lot of friends and was making a little money. I had a car and a girlfriend for the first time. She was a lovely blond girl named Sue. I was a fraternity president. I was at a personal pinnacle of success and drank a lot.

When I was eighteen or nineteen, I started to look at the world around me and decide what I wanted to do. I broke the world down into five categories: where I lived, where I worked, my social situation, my sexual situation, and finally my financial situation. I would use my skills to improve each category.

It was pretty sad.

I figured if my outsides were okay, my insides would be okay. I didn't know anything from my skin on in, nothing about my life, and nothing about who I was. My life had been given over to social deception. I was good at that.

I had no clue about my relationship to a Higher Power. As a child, when I'd gone with a friend to a catechism class, I found it strange. I had no curiosity whatever.

With nothing to go on, I started to formulate ideas about religion. I hammered them out in a bar where I'd find myself getting into violent arguments about religion and spirituality, things I knew nothing about.

My college years were validated only by my social skills. I had friends. I was in with the gang, which was good because I was needy. However, I chose not to notice how needy I was for approval.

When it came to money, when it came to women, I had nothing at all inside to sustain me. My neediness turned to desperation.

My self-reliance wasn't making it.

I had no defense against the first drink. Once I had taken it, alcohol took on a life of its own. My friends were all hanging out in bars. I hung up my hat in a bar, and that's where it stayed. One by one, my friends would mature, go back to school, get married, and move on.

But I stayed and did bar jobs to pay my tab. This is something that usually happens farther down the line. You'll see guys, swampers, who do nothing but menial bar work.

I'd move in with a woman for a couple of months, then get thrown out. Then I'd go home and stay with my parents. If I didn't blame them for my life, it was only because blame wasn't fashionable yet. I was willing to suggest that my parents hadn't developed me properly.

My father was a meek man who didn't want the world poking fun at him. At least that's how I saw him. He wasn't an aggressive male who brought home the bacon. With the little college education I had and a few buzz words, God help me, I was able to blame my parents.

(Yes, the mother whose leg I'd clung to, who'd kept me safe by her presence.)

My parents were poor and needed every dime they could get, but during those years I never did a thing to help them. I never even thought about helping them. I'd live with them, eat their food, and never contribute a dime.

My self-centeredness consumed me, and my drinking was making me angry. When I didn't feel a part of a group, I'd choose not to participate. My driving got angrier, and I got into the court system for drunk driving. I stopped going to my Naval Air Reserve meetings.

My boss was calling me in and friends were pulling me aside.

My parents were disappointed. I was just drinking, which is a good man's failing.

Finally, the military had enough and decided to send me to Vietnam. Prior to that, I'd met a young lady who was interested in me. She thought she'd have a good man if she could get me away from my friends and the booze. So we got married.

I stood at God's altar and said the vows (which I think are the deepest things you can say to another human being). Then I got on my aircraft carrier a few weeks afterward for Vietnam. The first port we hit was Hawaii, where I drank and whored. The same in the Philippines, Japan, and everywhere else we landed. I didn't even think of honoring my vows.

On my return, she was still waiting for me. We tried to hammer out a life, but I went on drinking. My wife gradually became like a fawn in a forest fire. Finally, she proved to be more intelligent and divorced me.

"How could she do this to me," I thought, "after all I've done for her?"

I felt I'd been working hard my whole life. Now I didn't have two nickels to show for it. I decided to drop out of the world. I took to the streets. That went on for three or four years. It was blurred from drinking. Life on the streets lasted until I was thirty-eight years old. A blurred street and a blurred life—that was the bottom.

A boyhood friend and drinking buddy I hadn't seen in a while had been through the courts for drunk driving and been sentenced to AA. He was a shy, timid guy, and he asked if I'd go to AA with him. I'd go to AA because he needed it.

That's how I got to my first meeting, February 15, 1976.

I was a mess. I only went to help him out. But where you hurt most and what you fear most are the closest places to God.

When I walked in, only to help my friend, it was the start of a spiritual adventure that has lasted twenty-six years.

I felt welcome. It was a miracle to me. I was used to being asked to leave places. Somebody took me by the arm, and I was so touched. I can't tell you how much. There was grace in the room.

The oddest thing resulted. I was suddenly enthusiastic. It seemed the world had become a new place where I was welcome, where I could look around. Now I had a place to go where I was wanted. I didn't have to be wary.

God comes in these strange and simple ways. It's like the world turns upside down. I went to a lot of meetings. I averaged one, two, even three a day. Once, on a very bad day, I attended six meetings. Through that process (they say that meetings are the way to the Way), I started to recognize the day-to-day mechanics of the spiritual.

I did what they told me and asked me to do. My sponsor was an old drinking buddy. He'd been a bartender. He knew all the games I could play. I asked him, "Well, what should I do?" He said, "Read the next line in the book." The next line read, "This defense must come from a power greater than ourselves."

I said, "That's interesting, but what does it mean? How do I get it?"

"The whole purpose here, Don, is to get to Step Twelve so you'll wake up spiritually. That will be your defense against the first drink."

He laid it out for me. It was the first time I had ever taken absolute direction. That's what I thought, anyway. Actually I'd been taking a lot of direction from my needs and fears. But this was different. It was the first time that I knew where I was in the world. I was on Step One and headed for Step Twelve, and I wasn't going to deviate for relationships, money, or vocation.

He told me that until I got where I was going, my defense was going to be other alcoholics and other human beings. I didn't have a job at that point, so I had seven meeting commitments, one for every day of the week.

I got a job and a place to live. My friend got me working with others. There was suddenly meaning in my life, and meaning is food.

I was frenzied for the next four or five years. I loved AA, helped newcomers, and spoke a little bit. I had a place in the world. I had taken direction from other people. God had talked to me in rooms full of people.

I met a wonderful lady who would become my wife. We were known as the Lady and the Tramp. The only thing we had in common was that she was a sorority girl and I knew a little bit about fraternities. We lived a marriage where we never had an argument. We opened up our house to newcomers who were floundering or needed help. When the kids would come home from school, there'd be somebody new in the house and they'd run up and introduce themselves. It helped heal, which is something that goes on all the time in everyone. The kids grew up in an atmosphere of sharing, loving, self-sacrifice, and giving back to the world. It's a fabulous way to live.

I *had* something. God was restoring me to sanity.

Not just helping me to stay sober, but restoring me to sanity, which is a scarcer quantity than we'd like to think.

It isn't just about sobriety. It's about life and a tenderness for it, waking up naked on God's green earth.

CHAPTER NINETEEN

All Substance

DIFFERENT VOICES coming back to the heart of things.

I like Don's voice because it isn't strained. He has little to say about his time on the streets because he knows it lacks meaning. If you asked, he'd tell you. If you ask about anything he knows, he'll tell you. There's a wonderful balance here—the things that hurt, the sudden waves of memory and humiliation, the occasional joy above happiness are all given their weight and place with no fuss at all, no "look at me, look at me."

The waves of regret and embarrassment you have to learn to handle. For three years, all I could do was put my head down and say, "Please help me."

Don rode his personality as far as it would go. It isn't much of a ride, and in that way lies hell. The personality blossoms, fills up the head, then dies slowly, fighting for life. It's a lot of effort to feel empty. It takes a lot of doing to reach the real thing. You're empty but there's something left.

There's something left: the light and the memory and the pulsing things, the thoughts and the churning and the feel of the heart rippling, the voice of the soul like a radio getting closer. You're emptied into the real, which is all substance.

I don't have a lot to say about Don's piece. He lives his life trying to pass on what he has, and he does it without any fuss, in perfect low-key grace.

He has nothing to forgive anyone for anymore, which is a great place to be, hoping only for your own forgiveness.

Which comes around as something like, "God, we all loved each other, didn't we?"

How do you get there? You pay attention. You see and listen closely. You walk.

The personalities shimmer and waver, but the core is the same. The souls are implacable, with all the patience of the endless.

These aren't people who stand up and scream, "I'm saved, Lord, I'm saved." These are people who come to the point of realization that they always had been saved, but they just hadn't noticed. More to the point, these aren't people who tell you how to live or how to think.

They don't condemn to hell. They don't exclude and make lists. They see clearly. They may get angry and may rage against the hierarchies of the unreal and the unmistakable smell of hypocrisy, but they don't pass on misery. They don't distort children and don't pretend to know.

They make the world a better place, insofar as they can.

❧

Kathleen isn't Don, but she's more like him than unlike, as are we all.

I met with her at her home, where all the colors are muted, pastels mostly, and the furnishings are simple and spare. The brightest colors are in the photographs of her daughter. The room feels almost meditative, maybe cloistered.

Kathleen is medium height and blond. She has a Doris Day look, without the makeup. She's forty-three years old and dresses simply in a skirt and blouse. Her manner of speech is absolutely straightforward. It would be hard to imagine her lying about anything.

She was once one of our children, the ones we talk about sentimentally but cut out of our budgets so not to pay as much in taxes.

Anyone who can't hear Kathleen is as lost as she once was.

CHAPTER TWENTY

Kathleen

I GREW UP in the town of Tiburon, which is one of the wealthiest places in the United States. When I was young my family was very wealthy—my dad was a union official. Because he was a drunk, we lost everything.

He left us when I was five or six. I only saw him once in a while after that. He left my mom with seven children under the age of ten and wiped out the bank account. He was a binge drinker. I remember the chaos and my mom getting us all together in our car, driving to my grandmother's house because my dad was on a rampage.

He'd chase my mother around the house. I remember coming home and seeing him lying on the couch all bloody because he had passed out drunk and driven a car through a fence and into a building.

He'd lock himself in his office and say he'd commit suicide. People called my mom in the middle of the night, asking to talk to him.

After he left, it was even scarier, because with my mom's codependency and her need to control everything, being overwhelmed with seven kids and having so much anger and resentment toward my dad, things got physically and verbally abusive in my house.

My dad sexually abused me and my sister. He basically made

me his wife. I can remember in my earliest memories falling asleep with him in my bed and waking up with him there. I couldn't tell anybody. I couldn't talk about it. Nobody in my family found out until much later, when I was a heavy alcoholic. My sister told my mom what had happened.

My mom was a rageaholic. She had to work really hard to support all us kids, and when she got home late at night she'd wake us up, empty all our drawers, and hit us with frozen meat. It was terrifying.

What I began to learn was that the world was not safe, and there was no soft place to fall, and I didn't deserve to be protected. If we had been a TV sitcom, it would have been called "The Look-Good Family." But everything was chaos, on the outside. . . .

Our mother sent us to Catholic school. I went to Saint Hilary's. We learned about a God who was frightening and shaming, and that we should always feel guilt. We were hit a lot with yardsticks. We were supposed to be good little soldiers.

We were treated differently after my dad left. We became the poor family in the really rich community. People knew what was going on even though my mom didn't think they did.

She always told us they didn't know what was going on. We were supposed to take heart and believe that everything was okay because no one knew what we were really like.

My mom still thinks our dad's alcoholism didn't affect us because he did his drinking away from the house. That just shows you the nature of her codependency. It was all very hard, and I started feeling different from everyone else. Actually, it seemed to be clear that we were different.

I was supposed to get awards at the end of the school year because I was the straight A student. I was seeking approval from my teachers and looking for any validation as a human being. Instead, they gave all the awards to the rich kids and didn't give any to me. My mom sat there crying.

Once again, I felt like it was my fault, because in an alcoholic home you learn not to feel your own feelings. You learn to be responsible for your alcoholic parent's feelings and your co-dependent parent's feelings.

We were told, "You kids are what's ruining my life. You kids are what's giving me these headaches." I worried, "How is Mom going to be when she gets home?" We walked on eggshells all the time and felt responsible. It was our fault that her life was ruined, that our dad had left.

The first time I drank was in the summer of seventh grade with kids from school. We went up on a hill. I think I told my mom I was spending the night at a friend's house. Somebody had a bottle of Red Mountain wine.

The big secret in my house had been well kept. My dad's denial of his alcoholism went on for many years. It was the dirty secret. I didn't know then what alcohol would do to *me,* though I'd seen what it did to my father. Who cared? I didn't much like who I was, and what could be worse than that?

The kids brought out the bottle. I didn't sip it like the others; I chugged it. I gulped down half a bottle of wine and went into a blackout.

When I woke up, I was in the most popular boy's sleeping bag. All I remembered was that when I drank alcohol it didn't taste good, but that once it got down I got a warm feeling. I felt I was as good as the kids I was with. I felt like I was with my peers.

I felt pretty, witty, and I knew that everything was just right. I felt okay in my skin, at least until I blacked out, and after that, who knew?

For the next three days rooms spun around me as I threw up. I never wanted to drink again, and I didn't, for three years. Instead, I smoked pot and took hallucinogens.

In addition, I got put into foster homes because the abuse in my house was so bad. My mom actually kicked me out at one point. She didn't want me because I was a reminder of my father.

When she kicked me out, I didn't have anywhere to live, which is why they put me in a foster home. I'd leave there and stay at different friends' houses. Sometimes I'd be homeless on the street, sleep in garages with newspaper over me, or find car doors left open so I could sleep in the backseat.

I was put into another foster home where the parents were addicts. They enrolled me in high school again. When I got back from school one day, they had a man in my bed. I had to get in with him and have sex.

When I refused to do that anymore, my foster mother threw me against a brick wall and I suffered head injuries. I was beat up pretty bad.

I was put in another foster home, which was pretty normal, but I had no idea how to function in a normal home with rules, love, and structure. I was so afraid. I had no idea what to do.

I ran away again, and this time nobody came for me. My mom might have told the authorities that I was at home with her so that they wouldn't look for me. If I was found, I was just a problem to her.

I had started drinking again and developed a body that seemed particularly attractive to older men, especially rock stars and drug dealers. I was living on the street, but I met some of them. My first real boyfriend was a guitar player.

Basically, I lived with guys like him from age fifteen to twenty-one. They had money because they had drugs. My drugs of choice were alcohol and cocaine. I needed them. I'd go anywhere, do anything, to get them.

Early on, when I was fifteen, I went with some older people to Lake Tahoe. They got a room at the casino, and after they'd all passed out from Quaaludes, I went downstairs. A guy came up and asked me what I was doing. I said I wanted to find a nightclub to go dancing, and he said he'd take me.

Well, he didn't take me to a nightclub. Instead, he took me to a hotel where he was staying. On the way there, he put his arm around my neck and said if I fought with him, he'd kill me. He raped me and drove me back to the casino. I didn't tell any of the security guards because I thought they'd put me in jail, since I was a runaway. The people I was with didn't believe me, so I used the phone and called the mother from the healthy foster family. She sent me a bus ticket to get home.

When I got there, I didn't go to her house. Instead, I went to a drug dealer's house.

I did geographical cures.

I was doing cocaine. I thought, "I'll move to Hawaii, it's just the place. It's healthy and sunny and I won't do drugs there." That was my best thinking. I got money from a guy, bought a plane ticket, and went to Hawaii with three cents left in my pocket. On the plane, I met a drug dealer and went home with him.

But he sold only pot and I needed my cocaine. So I applied for a job as a cocktail waitress. It wasn't just a waitress job, but a strip club. I was mortified. I was still a Catholic girl, even though I had no faith in God. If there was a God, why was my life so miserable? My mom had told me that if there was a God, her life wouldn't have been ruined so bad.

Why did my dad leave us like that? "Never trust men or God," Mother said. I remember her saying that.

Anyway, I took the job and remember what it took for me to be a stripper. I had to get really drunk. I would drink double shots of 151 Brown, top shot, and pineapple juice. I was so drunk that I was holding myself up on the pole you're supposed to be swinging around on stage. I couldn't even see the people in the audience.

One night one of the girls turned me on to some little white pills called cross tops, speed. If I took some with alcohol, I wouldn't get so sloppy and could go for hours. In Hawaii, bars are open till four in the morning, and you only had to be eighteen years old. I had a fake ID.

I got an apartment with two other girls from the strip club. We'd go to work together, get drunk, and do speed. Then I couldn't get to sleep, so they gave me Seconals or reds. I was on a cycle of alcohol, speed, and Seconal.

I was so ashamed of myself. The incomprehensible demoralization of that job!

I got paid a lot, though. Guys would come from Pearl Harbor and spend their whole paychecks. A lot of them had never been away from home before. Many were virgins. A lot of them asked me to marry them.

Thank God I said no. I was already destroying my own life. I didn't need to take on someone else's.

One night when I took the Seconals, I couldn't remember how many I'd already taken. That morning, they couldn't wake me up. They put me in a cold bath and walked me around. I didn't have to go to the hospital, but it was a wake-up call. We all decided to quit stripping.

I don't know if it was a moment of clarity, but we all went to Maui and had fun. The others decided to leave, but I decided to stay because I'd met some new drug dealers and partiers who'd invited me to stay.

I had a boyfriend I thought was the greatest because he could drink while driving, throw up out the window, drink more, and keep on driving. He repelled a part of me. Another part of me thought he was great.

I got into the habit of manipulating guys, getting their car keys, and stealing their cars. The Maui authorities called my mom after I crashed a car during a blackout and told them somebody needed to come and get me.

When one of my sisters came, I went back to the mainland. I got deeper into cocaine and alcohol. What blows me away is how long I went without dying or getting locked away in a mental ward. I'd been to emergency psychiatric care units a number of times. I had seizures, and cocaine made me paranoid.

In 1982, when I was twenty-six, I went to a club looking for drugs and for guys to buy me drinks. When I got back in my car, somebody put a knife to my throat from the backseat. I had to follow another car with two other guys in it.

They kidnapped me and for two days sexually and physically abused me, pistol-whipped me, and eventually left me for dead in a ravine.

By the grace of God, two hikers found me. My jaw was broken; my whole body was broken. I was black and blue. I stayed at a hospital for a while.

The men were arrested and put in jail. But when I got out, my boyfriend told me that I couldn't testify in court because he was a coke dealer and it would bring the cops around. He didn't want me to talk about the rapes, either, because it made him think less of me. So I internalized and started having anxiety attacks. The men had been set loose, and I thought they were going to kill me. They had been arrested for a few other things when the police showed up. They had drugs and weapons and headed up a pimping ring in San Francisco.

They were in trouble for all of that, but they didn't have to go to trial for the rape and kidnapping. It was on the front page of the local newspaper, which was awful and humiliating. I was getting to be *the victim*. I'd been beat up a bunch of times, and this had been the second series of rapes.

I think God tries to get your attention by throwing a pebble at you, then a rock, and then a boulder. This was my boulder, and I wish I could say I got it then, but I didn't. I tried to commit suicide three months later. I was in a coma for a while. I wanted to die. I couldn't numb myself anymore.

I suffered not just from what the men had done to me, but from the memories of my childhood, of my father, of Tahoe—everything. A volcano was erupting inside me.

The doctors told my boyfriend that there was no reason I was alive after all the drugs I'd ingested. I'd taken sixty pills, along with huge amounts of cocaine and alcohol. There's no reason a human being with that much toxicity should have survived.

No matter. I got out of the hospital and started drinking and using to make the pain go away. I started my geographical cures again. I got jobs that I thought might limit my drinking. I hung out with lower companions. I became a lower companion. I'd wake up in my house with men I didn't know. In the end, I couldn't be alone. I needed somebody near me, even if it was a stranger. A warm body next to me was all I needed.

I'd be on the couch, then roll onto the floor and not feel the pain. Drunks either die, go insane, or get locked up. I did all of those. I did seven months in jail when I stole a car in Nevada.

I didn't call anyone for help because I knew that I didn't deserve help. I didn't believe I could be helped.

I was living in a town called Occidental in my folks' vacation house, and I'd been up all night. I don't know why it happened, but out of nowhere I opened the phone book and looked under drugs.

This was a time when rehab was not popular or spoken about. I'd never heard about AA or recovery. Nothing was listed under drugs, so I looked up alcohol.

It was a moment of clarity. I called the number I found. A man named George answered. He asked me my name, and I said, "Kathleen Victoria."

"Do you know, Kathleen Victoria, that you never have to drink again?"

"Really," I said.

I couldn't believe it. And he said, "Or use again. You never have to drink or do drugs again." It astounded me. His was the first voice. I'd become resigned to the fact that I had no will-power to resist drinking or drugs.

The man told me that I could go there, go through their detox, and maybe afterward go through their twenty-eight-day program. I was completely willing. I checked in and went through detox for a week. I was really, really sick.

At the first meeting outside of detox, I saw the Steps on the wall, the word *God,* and I thought, "This won't work for me. If there was a God, my life wouldn't be like this. God wouldn't have let all these things happen. How dare they say there's a God?"

When I saw the Eighth and Ninth Steps about making amends, I couldn't think of any amends I needed to make. Everyone had done everything to me. I was a victim. Things were being done to me, and it was everyone else's fault.

When I heard the others tell their stories, I heard hope. So I finished the program, learned about getting a sponsor, and worked the Steps. They told me I had to pray. I didn't want to pray. When I finally did, I was swearing like a sailor.

"They say I have to pray to you, Motherfucker God, and I don't believe you're there, but they say I have to do it."

My roommate in rehab said she would laugh under her covers because I was so funny, praying while being so angry. Maybe it was cute, but it wasn't to me. I didn't believe in God at all.

I did come to believe in a power greater than myself. I suppose I didn't have much trouble with that, because what power had there ever been that wasn't greater than mine? I got a sponsor and slowly but surely began to find faith.

At first it was just in the group, but as I did things and got in a woman's meditation group, everything changed. I felt a weight disappearing and felt somehow a loving God who just wanted his kids to be happy.

It wasn't about shame and guilt and fear. I found a different God than the one they'd given me as a child. I got into volunteer service, answered the phones, and became employable. I went to college and got a nursing degree. I listened to what people told me.

Around five years sober, I got some outside therapy that my sponsor had suggested to deal with the childhood abuse, rapes, and beatings. It was overwhelming. I couldn't cope. I went into a state where I thought every man was my father; every man was one of the men who had raped me.

I was ready to blow my brains out. I had a gun, and I got a bottle of alcohol and drank. After I drank, I called my sponsor and my sister; they took me to the hospital.

The doctor said there was no physical reason I was vomiting

blood, that it seemed to be from emotional pain. I was there for about a week, vomiting blood. When I got out, I didn't want anything to do with AA, because I felt that they had failed me and that God had failed me. I think now I had kept a part of myself from God, a part I couldn't trust anyone with. The terror was so great from the sexual abuse; I hadn't been able to trust completely.

Do I think I did my best? Yes, I think I did my best.

It took a year for me to get back and two years for me to get sober.

I managed to lose my money, my house, everything, and I moved to the East Bay with a Hell's Angel. I was his property. I was owned, beaten, and back in my role as a victim.

When I was lost completely, I had to go back to AA. It was the only place where I knew they'd take me. Even though I was full of rage, anger, and bitterness against them, I knew that if I wanted to live I had to go back. I was having seizures.

I got out of the East Bay and went back to Sonoma County, where I'd gone through rehab. I went to some meetings. The first night I was back was New Year's Eve, 1991. I found a man and took him hostage. Oh, we took each other hostage. We were both very sick. Ten months later, I married him. He was a violent man, and I got beaten a lot for no reason.

There was just a part of me that wouldn't heal. I was holding back.

That was the wounded part. I couldn't go near it.

The relationship progressed just like the disease. I was married and pregnant and being beaten. I only left him because I loved my baby. I couldn't leave him. I loved the baby inside. Despite the abuse and the alcohol, by the grace of God my baby was born without any problems. Well, she had a few problems.

She was premature, but had no problems that were alcohol related.

I wasn't supposed to be able to have children. Because of the rapes, I'd been ripped up real bad. Having my daughter was the beginning of coming back.

I wish I could say I jumped right back into the program, but I didn't. I isolated myself. The pregnancy was the loneliest, scariest time of my life. I was full of anger and resentment, but eventually I started coming out of it and working the program.

I was introduced to Al-Anon, which gave me a place to talk about addiction and family and growing up. I opened up slowly. I'd been told many times, "Don't talk about being abused; men don't want women who're abused."

My family pretended none of it had ever happened. They said I was crazy and made it up. To them, I was really nothing at all, nothing. But in Al-Anon I could talk. I got into outside therapy again and began to deal with it. I'm still dealing with it.

Just before I went back to AA for the last time, I was very sick and couldn't sleep. I said, "Jesus" (I have no idea why I said "Jesus"), "if you are there, please put me to sleep tonight."

And I fell asleep.

The next night, I couldn't sleep again. I kept thinking about how I'd have to get up to take my little girl to school, and I remembered. I said, "Jesus, please, put me to sleep. Jesus, if you're there, please put me to sleep."

And I fell asleep.

One of the moms at my daughter's school told me about a church she went to. I started to go. It was a Christian church, and I didn't believe in Jesus Christ or any of that, but I went because I felt that something had heard me. I started going to this church, and slowly I began to believe again.

Then last year I got really sick. I was diagnosed with cancer and needed chemotherapy. During the chemo, I had a huge spiritual awakening. I think I got so defenseless from being sick that I couldn't maintain the guard around my heart.

Everything came back to me, the physical abuse and the rape, and I was lying on the couch, too weak to stand and hardly able to lift my head. Suddenly feelings flooded me. My guard was down, and I was too weak to fight, to push the feelings down. I knew the shame and fear were blocking me from God. A dam broke inside me, and all my feelings flooded up. I started crying and I said, "Thank you, Lord, for healing. Thank you. Thank you, Lord."

From that point on, I was free. That's the best way I can describe it. No more bondage. I knew I'd be okay. Today I live a life of freedom I never could have imagined.

I'm a good mother. My daughter's never seen me drunk. My health has kept me from working, but I hope I can go back to work soon. I can be a good mother, friend, and woman. I feel valuable because I belong to the human race, and I contribute.

I go to church and take my daughter so she can learn about a loving and forgiving God. We pray together every day, every night, and I have my meditations. I can't lose what I have unless I choose to.

I've been given so much that I can't imagine giving it all away. And I have so much more, so much more, when I stop to feel it.

I'm really glad to be able to share this with you. I'm really grateful, because I barely existed for so long. I just want to tell you that you can recover from anything, and I want to thank you.

CHAPTER TWENTY-ONE

How Did That Happen?

SHE WENT BACK to her family and they didn't believe her. Why?

Was it inconvenient? Did they not believe her because it would mean looking at the past? Because it might hurt? Because someone might have to accept responsibility? Because someone might have to be forgiven?

There it is again. The inherited wretched wisdom of misery and addiction and humanity. "We're different, and there is no love for us."

If no one in the world had come to God save Kathleen, her voice would cut through all the other cant. Her daughter probably won't be like she was, so the sum total of human misery will have decreased. How will that have happened?

"When she got home late at night she'd wake us up, empty all our drawers, and hit us with frozen meat. It was terrifying."

Isn't this just what God does, if you believe the hierarchies and the dogma? He comes into our lives at night, rummages through our secrets, empties all our drawers, and beats us for our dereliction, our dirty magazines, our failures of doctrine and self-loathing.

Believe is the key word. We assume that the mind is capable of amassing knowledge adequate for belief. In fact, what's based in belief is based in a shifting, hallucinogenic swamp where reason makes paths leading anywhere and nowhere, and somewhere there's a God who rages against us and beats us up for all eternity.

The sad truth is that it is easier for someone who doesn't believe to come to God than it is for someone who does believe. The nonbeliever hasn't taken any wooden nickels yet, and can feel and be bathed in God without the fear of doing something wrong, of saying the wrong thing, of not kissing the hem of the robe.

The mind is perfectly capable of defending the purely mental judgments that come from a place of utter vanity and personality, the structures that reek of the lust for power, the rationalizations of hypocrisy, and the hidden need for revenge.

The mind held in grace can do none of that, and wouldn't if it could.

I know a woman who kicked her fifteen-year-old daughter out of the house because she'd gotten pregnant, reminding her of what *she'd* done when *she* was sixteen. "She had to learn," she said. "She needed to listen to me in my own house."

She believed she was being reasonable. And so we pass on false beliefs, destructive reasoning. Reason is nothing without love. Logic is a baleful thing if not informed and balanced by emotion understood and expressed. We seem to believe that the mind keeps the unruly emotions in check. Actually, the emotions informed by love are infinitely more reliable than reason, which can successfully rationalize and defend any crime, any cruelty.

If you remember being very young, if you remember that there was no cruelty you were drawn to, then you know that before reason comes the heart.

I love Kathleen because she's human and because she offers herself as an opening into God. I don't *believe* in her. That would imply that it would be possible *not* to believe in her.

"God's love for us isn't the reason we should love Him," Simone Weil says. "God's love for us is reason for us to love ourselves. What other reason could we have for loving ourselves?"

Kathleen knows this.

❧

I've known Alfred, the last to speak in this book, for a long time.

He was a demon of sorts. He had a manic intensity, and his theatricality was overpowering. His voice rolled and boomed and the words were florid, though always to the point. He was a fine actor, though he never managed to achieve what he could have. He drank a great deal and took whatever drug happened to be around.

He's sixty now, and after years of sobriety, lapses, working with Mother Teresa's people, episodes with the police, teaching at a reservation, motorcycle accidents, volunteer jobs, worrying the edges of the church, taking up with the wrong people, and hiding in the psychoanalytic jargon of the fifties, he's come to rest—not too well physically but much better in every other way.

He's average height and has always been muscular. The voice that boomed and rolled is much subdued, because he has emphysema. Once to be feared, his wit is less aggressive.

In college, he stole the Christ child from the crèche in the town square. When they came to get him, he was sitting in a pizza parlor with the baby on the table. He'd put one of his gloves on the infant's hands with the middle finger stuffed with toilet paper to keep it stiff.

In the seventies, when he was living in Woodstock with his brother, both of them alcoholic, he called the police one evening because they'd had a drunken fight. The police took his brother away. When they finally let him go, he killed himself.

Alfred's voice isn't just subdued. It has a hundred years of weariness in it, and an almost gentle surprise. The quality of expression is intense, sometimes stabbing.

I wish you could actually hear the voice. It has the full, tonal weight of acceptance and beauty.

CHAPTER TWENTY-TWO

Alfred

MY NAME IS ALFRED, which has never been for me a clear thing to say. But I can sit here now with everything, heading away in all directions, and I can sit and be calm and still and know that at this moment everything *is* still. At this moment everything is in balance . . . at this moment.

For the first time in my life, I'm happy and calm. It's taken me a little while to reach this point. When I used to look back at my life, at all the waste and carnage, I was convinced that my life was over and the loss was irredeemable. I rued the loss of my facile mind and the loss of my gifts. There was, as someone once wrote in a book, a leftover life to kill.

However grandiose it may sound, standing on the precipice, being dramatic, about to plunge, well, you know, I'd much rather sit here and smoke this cigarette. Gradually, I've come to have a new point of view about my life. It just changed.

I have different satisfactions in life now. I enjoy working as a volunteer for various organizations, doing very simple things. I mean, when I was drinking, I led a delusional life. I was running from myself because I didn't know who I was, and I couldn't solve that intellectually. My feelings were pretty much numbed, for whatever reasons.

I came from an alcoholic home, a lot of miscommunication and noncommunication, a lot of unspoken thoughts—in some sense always secret. There were secrets about myself that for some reason I couldn't tell myself.

I thought that I was an artist. That was the one thing I was sure of. I was an artist. I wanted to be an artist. I started writing at fourteen. I remember my first poem, some images from it. I don't know, it just calmed me. It was something I felt I'd done right.

I remember standing with some of my high school friends at a bar when I was somewhere around sixteen years old. We were drinking and talking about my poem. I would run to alcohol with a flow of feeling, but my poems were never about a flow of feeling. They were always abstracted from who I really was. Maybe they were attempts to find out who I really was, I don't know. In any event, I became a fairly self-obsessed person, and a very dramatic one. I cultivated eccentricities.

If there was one thing I didn't want to be it was an ordinary, normal person. I found people like that boring and dull. I was going to win an Academy Award for being eccentric. I don't know. I just was a very confused kid, and I went deeper and deeper into the unknown, into the chaos of not knowing, and that satisfied me. It created explosions within myself and my personality. I was the debris. Remember, I was driven by my bi-polar problem and driven by alcohol. I was actually a very frightened person. I could pretend to be brave, and nobody would know I was fear-laden.

All this running away as a result of fear. I don't feel particularly afraid of things right now. I can't say that completely. Well, I guess I'm afraid of people. I'm really *not* afraid of death. I accept the fact that my memories are deteriorating, and I accept the fact that my body is deteriorating. I think it's one of those jokes the cosmos plays on you.

I finally have a handle on my spirituality. I'm not as arrogant as I was. I try to replace it with humility. It's not so much substituting, but more an organic process. Things that have happened to me that were a part of my fate. Some things helped. What I needed, I went out and got.

Quality of life is most important to me. Quality of life for me is knowing who I am and being able to mix with my fellow beings on the planet. I make that a process that encourages the growth of everyone I come around. I hope I'm making myself to some degree understandable, but that's what I mean by quality of life. It's compassion and loving-kindness.

I've become a Buddhist, and not a particularly fervent kind. There is a great deal of value there for me. I do have my moments of meditation, and my basic approach to life is a meditative one—so far as I'm able to keep my awareness from limping off into the night and becoming vague and nuts.

The center of my being is simplicity, kindness, and mindfulness. I don't just say what comes into my head without it having some kind of sense of appropriateness. I'm trying to overturn the chaotic, self-indulgent behaviors of the first part of my life. Those behaviors were in some ways randomly cruel behaviors. This happens by the process of breath and awareness of the space around me and of the beings in that space. I find that harmony is possible and that I no longer have this concern to make witty remark upon witty remark upon witty remark, often at the expense of other people. I don't have to be top dog and keep everyone at bay because I'm afraid somebody would find out who I am. I *don't know* who I am, and sometimes I've been afraid that maybe there's nothing there.

During my last manic-depressive episode, I wound up drinking, and it left me broken and exhausted. I'm going to be sixty years old next month, and that last episode took place earlier this year, in January. I was just completely exhausted by it. I had no choice but to surrender to the force of my disease and ultimately to turn it over to a Higher Power. I just didn't have any other option. I was just rotten and rancid. I don't know how else to describe it. Taking a single step felt like a column of troops moving into a sandstorm. I can't come up with an adequate image.

I was a rebel without a cause. I only had fear. I was a rebel, but I had nothing to rebel against because everything was in a desert where the wind plucks dead stuff out of the sand and blows it around. I was blowing around. I wanted only rest and peace.

There's nothing for me to do right now. I've got a rich and full life. Maybe I'll go to some meetings again. And not be the jackanapes on the high wire I used to play. I want every contact to be a spiritual contact. I'm subdued and quiet.

A lot of my life is taken up by seeing doctors, keeping my days rolling. I want to simplify my life. There's nothing to be gained in persisting in old patterns. I used to do this insane dance in a kind of trance.

I would drink and act on whatever impulse. I can remember doing things that were just so awful.

So right now I'm relieved to just sit and breathe and let the images come and fly away again. Thoughts come and just fly away. I've written a book of poems. I don't think I really have much to say, though I don't think that's very important.

I'm attached to my book, the idea that I have a book, but I wouldn't cling to the idea of art over the simplicity I have in my life now.

I have not said things consecutively. Neither have I spoken well, but if this happens to help or inform anyone who reads this book, I'm glad. Maybe someone will stop to think, "Well, I'm kind of like that. I sort of understand what he's talking about. Maybe I should stop all the bullshit and just get simple, try and deal with people." I mean, if a word here touches another's consciousness of heart, soul, or being, that'll be worth it all.

It's a fellowship. People help one another.

I have no regrets about this opportunity missed or about that lost acreage of time. I'm just happy to be sitting here recording this for a friend who may or may not put it in a book. Whatever happens with my health, I'm very glad to be sitting here, talking spontaneously, trying to come clean.

If it goes no farther than my speaking into this tape, that's good because it clarifies my conscience and my consciousness both. I could go on, but I won't. I've said everything I wanted to say, however badly.

To quote Tiny Tim (which was never me, which was never something I would have done), "God bless us, everyone."

Good-bye.

Epilogue

WE WANT TO THANK everyone who offered a life to this book. It was our hope that in the flow of a number of stories the basic outline of a movement toward God might become visible. In all of these narratives there's a core of surrender, a place where the personality gives up and the mind gives up and the relaxed body feels something *other*—a touch, a sudden access to breath, an opening of the chest, a sheet of crazed tears.

The surrender is a sudden understanding of one's own strength, because it isn't a giving up to force, brutality, or Caesar—to surrender to Caesar is to surrender to a lesser power. The true surrender is to the good, which brings with it strength, calm, and a surge of astonished being. "Oh, yeah, here I am. Oh God, thank you."

Whether the surrender is to the sudden feeling of identity with other human beings—singing together, rising out of themselves—or to the realization that all our best efforts and best works of mind have brought us to misery and a place where we can't stop wretchedly inflicting misery on others, it's the same quantity, a convulsion of mechanical, predictable, and rationalized half-life.

When these habits of being and seeing break, you can hear and feel the soul. And the soul always touches God—calmly, implacably.

Thanks again to everyone. It's been a pleasure.

About the Authors

Jack Erdmann
An accomplished salesman and businessman, Jack Erdmann is also an author and lecturer in the San Francisco area. A fourth-generation alcoholic, he has been sober for more than twenty-five years.

Larry Kearney
Larry Kearney was born in Brooklyn in 1943, moved to San Francisco in 1964, and has since published eleven books of poetry. He had his last drink in 1981.